PRAISE FOR
ADD: HELPING
YOUR CHILD

p.134

An Alternate Selection of Teacher Book Club

❑

"The authors have done an excellent job of presenting a comprehensive, accurate, and readable book. As a pediatrician, I plan to recommend the book to every family in my practice who is dealing with ADD. I particularly like the frequent outline format and recommendations for parents and teachers. It is the best book on ADD I have seen."

—J. Patrick Morrison, M.D.

❑

"A valuable resource for parents, teachers, and mental health professionals. The authors have distilled a vast amount of information regarding this highly controversial, yet common, disorder, into a highly readable and instructive book. The reader is provided with numerous proven strategies. Parents will become more effective advocates for their child. Teachers will understand the problem and work with the child more successfully, and other professionals will gain greater sensitivity and understanding of the parents' and child's perspectives."

**—Nick Elksnin, Ph.D., NCSP; school
psychologist**

❑

more...

"Umansky and Smalley provide good examples of how ADD affects children at school and at home and helpfully outline specific strategies for building success for children and their families. This book reassuringly acknowledges and supportively encourages the vital role that parents play not only in helping their children but in educating schools to serve children with ADD appropriately."

—Irene Wood, critic, editor, and parent of two children with ADD

❑

"Among the great strengths of this book is the authors' sensitivity to the needs of these children...and most importantly the critical message that parents of children with ADD must not lose sight that ultimately it is the bond between parents and children that best predicts their emotional health and future well-being."

—Sam Goldstein, Ph.D., author of *Managing Attention Disorders in Children*

❑

"Clinically precise and unusually clear, this book is filled with fresh, straightforward, practical strategies to help relax the knot in those of us who are touched by this disorder. The compassion and empathy with which this guide is written also helps loosen the knot. I am encouraged by the empathy that Dr. Umansky displays for the child, the parent, and also for the educators. I am encouraged by his reminders to be consistent with your children, to take time for yourself so you can relax, and to celebrate your children and their uniqueness."

—L. McGill, parent

❑

ADD:
Helping
Your Child

Untying the Knot of
Attention Deficit Disorders

WARREN UMANSKY, Ph.D., AND
BARBARA STEINBERG SMALLEY

WARNER BOOKS

A Time Warner Company

The material on pages 22–24 is reprinted with permission from the *DSM-IV Draft Criteria (3/1/93)*. Copyright © 1993 American Psychiatric Association.

Warner Books, Inc., 1271 Avenue of the Americas, New York, NY 10020

(w) A Time Warner Company

Printed in the United States of America

First Printing: July 1994

10 9 8 7 6 5 4 3 2 1

Library of Congress Cataloging-in-Publication Data
Umansky, Warren.
    ADD : helping your child / by Warren Umansky and
Barbara Steinberg Smalley.
      p.   cm.
    Includes bibliographical references and index.
    ISBN 0-446-67013-8
    1. Attention-deficit hyperactivity disorder—Popular works.
I. Smalley, Barbara Steinberg.   II. Title.
RJ506.H9U46   1994
618.92'8589—dc20   93-33559
                                         CIP

Cover Design by Julia Kushnirsky
Cover photo by Richard Cohen
Book design by H. Roberts

We dedicate this book with deep appreciation to the children, parents, and teachers who have taught us so much, and to our families, who have provided love and support during our endeavors.

Special thanks to Donna R. Watson for her assistance and contributions to this project.

—*Warren Umansky*
Barbara Steinberg Smalley

WARREN UMANSKY, PH.D., is a child development specialist in private practice in Augusta, Georgia, and a consultant with Head Start as well as several schools and hospitals. He is the coauthor of *Young Children with Special Needs* and has published numerous research articles on related topics.

BARBARA STEINBERG SMALLEY is a writer whose articles have appeared in *New Woman, McCall's, Redbook, Family Circle, Cosmopolitan, Elle, Modern Bride, Bride's,* and *Woman's Day.* She is the coauthor of *More Power to You! How Women Can Communicate Their Way to Success.*

Dr. Umansky is available to lead seminars and workshops on ADD for parents and professionals. For more information contact: Barbara Steinberg Smalley, 220 Ferncliff Drive, Athens, Georgia 30606.

How I feel

When I'm in class I don't
answer anything unless I'm
called on sometimes not
even then. I feel like it's just
an ordinary day like the rest.
It's like I'm never going to
remember anything at all never.
I feel worthless, useless,
like I'm stupid as heck
and I don't know anything.
I feel like nothing.
I FEEL
BLANK

That
is
what
I
feel.

—T.A.G., 12

Contents

INTRODUCTION
● ● ● ● ● ● ● ● ● ● ● ● ● ● ● ● ● ● ● ●
ADD:
The Misunderstood Disorder

Attention Deficit Disorders (ADD) affect between 3 and 10 percent of all school-age children. ADD is four to eight times more common in boys than it is in girls. It is the focus of thousands of recent scientific studies as well as a hot topic for magazines, newspapers, television talk shows, and newscasts.

ADD causes its young victims to be impulsive, easily distracted, and, in many instances, hyperactive. Undiagnosed and untreated, it wreaks havoc on a youngster's sense of self-esteem and interferes with his or her abilities to perform well at school, to make friends, and to get along with siblings and parents.

Children with ADD find themselves repeatedly reprimanded for doing things they can neither understand nor control. Caregivers and teachers may mistake such children's behavior and dismiss them as disruptive and uncooperative troublemakers. Parents of children with ADD often hold lofty expectations for their youngsters, expectations that are shattered by a child whose behavior they cannot seem to control. ADD can also zap the joy out of raising children, leaving parents of young victims often feeling humiliated, helpless, and wondering, "Where did we go wrong?"

Its roots are mysterious; its treatment is controversial. Despite the fact that it is one of the most prevalent childhood disorders, ADD remains one of America's most misunderstood maladies.

WHAT CAN I DO?

The comedian Martin Mull once said, "Having children is like having a bowling alley installed in your brain." Any household with children is destined to be chaotic, but one with a child who has ADD can be particularly tumultuous. Still, it doesn't have to be on par with a bowling alley, and that's where Chapter 4 ("A Home Program for Children with ADD") can help.

In this book, you will learn a number of strategies to help your child help himself. You will master new and effective ways to deal with the difficult behaviors that are characteristic of children with ADD. You will also learn how to deal with *your* needs as the parent of a child with this disorder.

Maybe your child attends school or a day-care center during the day, leaving you limited opportunities to spend quality time with her. Or maybe you stay at home with your preschooler and have increased contact with him. Regardless of your situation, the underlying philosophy of this book is: *However many or few hours you spend with your child, these times should be pleasant and productive, not marked by conflict and crisis.*

Granted, parenting is by nature a job filled with highs and lows. But you deserve to get satisfaction from your role, and our home program will show you how. Of course, no text can offer guarantees, but if you commit yourself to reading this book and following the recommendations consistently, you should experience many dramatic family changes. You will feel less frustration and anger when interacting with your child. Your child will feel more successful and experience an enhanced self-image. Finally, the way your entire family functions will change for the better. There will be less yelling, fewer threats made, a significant decrease in out-of-control emotional outbursts, and—best of all—greater pleasure in your role as a parent.

A significant part of this book will also be helpful to teachers, day-care personnel, and school administrators. Chapter 6, for example, is filled with strategies that can be used in the schools. In addition, other materials in the book will give professionals a better understanding of the problem of ADD from the perspective of the child and the parents. Being familiar with the material will allow parents and professionals to be on the same wavelength when they communicate about the needs of a particular child.

UNTYING THE KNOT

Finally, a word about the subtitle. The issues surrounding Attention Deficit Disorders are complex. They reach into the school, the community, and the family, as well as deep within the child's sense of accomplishment and self-esteem. They encompass academics, social skills, and vocational skills. We hope that this book, by offering you a greater understanding of ADD, provides a way to untie the knot that binds a very complex problem.

Many parents and caregivers describe a tightening in their stomach as they become increasingly frustrated and angry with their ADD children. By providing the tools both to deal with these frustrations and to redirect children with ADD in ways that will bring them greater success and less frustration, we hope to untie this knot as well.

1

• • • • • • • • • • • • • • • • • • • •

ADD:
What It Is
and Isn't

R obert, a third-grader, walks to school most days.
His school is no more than a five-minute trek
from home; yet even when Robert leaves on time,
he is often 30 minutes late.

His classmates don't like Robert very much. They say
he's bossy and claim he's always picking on them. Robert
has problems in the classroom as well. He spends the ma-
jority of his time under or near his desk rather than sit-
ting down and working. His handwriting is sloppy, his
work is messy, and his assignments are frequently left un-
finished. He's constantly losing things and can't seem to
keep up with the class when they are reading aloud. And

1

rarely does he have the right materials out to complete a given task.

At home Robert is equally disorganized. His parents say he is extremely messy and has to be repeatedly reminded to complete simple chores. In the neighborhood Robert has few friends his own age. When he plays with them, a fight typically ensues over sharing, hurt feelings, etc. Consequently Robert plays mostly with children who are older or younger than he is.

Robert was recently diagnosed as having Attention Deficit Disorder accompanied by hyperactivity. It used to be that slow learners and children who misbehaved, or who couldn't seem to pay attention in class, were considered mentally retarded, emotionally disturbed, or culturally disadvantaged. Research in the 1940s, however, turned up evidence of a fourth group: learning disabled children. The problems these youngsters had appeared to be neurologically based, and a new but equally degrading label—Minimally Brain Damaged—emerged with this discovery. In later years the term changed to Minimal Brain Dysfunction, then to Hyperkinetic Disorder of Childhood. A little more than a decade ago, the term Attention Deficit Disorders was coined to describe children who were not necessarily learning disabled but who were inattentive or hyperactive. In 1987 the term Attention Deficit Hyperactivity Disorder (ADHD) was added to differentiate between children with ADD who were not overly active and those with ADD who were also considered to be hyperactive.

WHAT IS ADD?

Attention Deficit Disorders was recently redefined by the American Psychiatric Association. The new definition describes two separate but related conditions. The first is characterized by chronic inattentiveness. For example, Robert rarely finishes his assignments in the classroom because he can't seem to pay attention long enough to complete them. When his class is reading aloud, he has trouble keeping up with them because his mind wanders. At home Robert's parents must repeatedly remind him to do his chores.

The second condition is characterized by hyperactivity and impulsiveness. In Robert's case, one of the reasons he is often late for school—even when he leaves on time—is that he might spot a frog along the way and decide to chase it for a while. Once in school, his teacher often calls out Robert's name because he is often under or near his desk rather than sitting down working. At home his parents say Robert rarely sits still, even when eating.

Considerable research over the past several years has focused on identifying the causes of ADD. The most recent evidence suggests that the level of neurological activity is quite different in certain parts of the brain in individuals with ADD compared to those who do not have the disorder. Furthermore, at least in some cases of ADD, these central nervous system differences appear to have a hereditary component.

WHAT IT'S NOT

ADD is a biological—*not* an emotional—disorder, though it can cause its victims to experience emotional problems at home, in school, and in social settings. Neither is ADD a learning disability, although many children with ADD also have learning disabilities.

In addition, many children with ADD exhibit obsessions and compulsions, symptoms of depression, enuresis (bed-wetting), tics, and other conditions. For the frustrated parent and the unhappy child, sorting out which symptoms are biologically based, which are learned behaviors, which are controllable or not controllable, and which are severe enough to interfere with the child's success, presents a significant dilemma.

Of course, not all youngsters who misbehave, who have trouble paying attention in school, or who have difficulty making friends have ADD. In fact, a host of physical, emotional, and situational problems can masquerade as ADD. Which is why it's imperative that a child be properly diagnosed before being treated.

DIAGNOSIS

ADD should be diagnosed by a team of professionals. Typically a medical doctor performs a thorough physical exam—which often includes neurological tests—to rule out any physical causes (such as vision problems or hearing loss) for the difficulties a child is experiencing. Next a psychologist evaluates the child's medical history, then solicits input from parents, teachers, and caregivers. Often the psychologist will also observe the child at school before suggesting a diagnosis.

What does the psychologist look for in the school setting? A number of characteristics that can support a diagnosis of ADD, as well as ideas to help the child improve his or her performance in the classroom. For example, the psychologist might note how the child's seat placement contributes to distractions and how it affects his ability to copy material from the chalkboard or get assistance from another child or the teaching staff. The psychologist will likely observe how much time the child spends paying attention to assigned work versus the amount of time spent daydreaming or working on other, unassigned tasks. She might observe how the child gets along with his peers, as well as the types of children he gets along with best—or worst.

The psychologist will likely monitor how successful the child is at paying attention to and completing independent work, and compare that to his performance in class discussions or in small groups. She will also note the frequency and intensity of the child's problem behavior—and how the teacher responds to the child. The psychologist may observe the child several times, on many different days.

The problem is that a child with ADD may show different behaviors in different settings, at different times of day, with different people, and when different levels of challenge are presented. Therefore relying on the report of one observer or formulating an impression of the child from an isolated observation may offer only a narrow view of the child's problem. For this reason, it is important to compare and contrast the child's performance under a number of conditions and to analyze observations from various individuals. You may be asked to fill out one or more behavior checklists, and to have your child's teacher or others do so. Professionals use these to help identify representative behaviors in your child as they complete an analysis of his performance. Some checklists specify the problem behaviors while others list the typical behaviors. Examples of these checklists are presented on pages 7 and 8.

When evaluating a child for ADD, psychologists and physicians rely on a profile of characteristics that tend to differentiate children who might have Attention Deficit Disorder from those who do not. Prior to the recent redefining of ADD into two groups—those who are inattentive and those who are hyperactive and impulsive—a group of fourteen symptoms was used to help diagnose the condition. Here is a list and a description of those symptoms:

CHARACTERISTICS OF ATTENTION DEFICIT DISORDER

Fidgets, Squirms, or Seems Restless

Children with ADD are often described as "always on the move." In the classroom, they are the pencil tappers or the ones who are constantly fiddling with other ob-

Behavior Checklist for Parents

Child's name_____age_____sex_____
Completed by: mother_____father_____other_____

Behavior	Not at all	Just a little	Pretty much	Very much
1. Runs or climbs excessively				
2. Trouble staying seated for meals or homework				
3. Fidgets excessively				
4. Doesn't finish work or tasks				
5. Doesn't work independently				
6. Doesn't seem to listen				
7. Easily distracted				
8. Acts before thinking				
9. Interrupts often				
10. Plays loudly				
11. Bossy or picks on other children				
12. Disliked by other children				
13. Shows poor self-esteem				
14. Disorganized				
15. Loses things needed for tasks				
16. Forgetful about school assignments and tasks				
17. Makes careless mistakes				
18. Has difficulty following directions				

Behavior Checklist for Teachers

Child's name_____age_____sex_____
Completed by: _____

Behavior	Not at all	Just a little	Pretty much	Very much
1. Completes seat work				
2. Pays attention				
3. Follows directions well				
4. Works well				
5. Stays on-task				
6. Is organized				
7. Thinks before acting				
8. Waits to be called on to respond				
9. Gets along with peers				
10. Awaits turn in games and groups				
11. Stays seated, as required				
12. Sits still				
13. Participates in group activities				
14. Controls emotions well				
15. Works carefully				

jects on their desks. At home, particularly during mealtime, they may toy with their silverware or food. Children with ADD also often demonstrate new and creative ways of sitting in a chair: on their legs, with legs propped up on a desk or table, etc.

Has Difficulty Remaining Seated

Teachers report that children with ADD are frequently out of their seats for a variety of reasons. They need a drink of water. They need to sharpen a pencil. They need to go to the bathroom. In fact, teachers say, it's not unusual to find a child with ADD wandering around the classroom for no apparent reason. At home a youngster with ADD usually eats on the go because he has a difficult time remaining seated for an entire meal. Homework time also suffers, because the child is unable to sit still long enough to complete his assignments. And when it comes to enjoying activities that require participants to sit for any length of time—such as concerts, lectures, and church or synagogue services—parents often resign themselves to the fact that they cannot take their ADD child along. If they do, they spend excessive amounts of time reminding him to remain seated and stay quiet.

Is Easily Distracted

Children with ADD lose their concentration very easily if there are sounds or movements around them. Consequently in school they have difficulty focusing on independent seat work if, for example, a reading group nearby is making noise. Homework becomes a chore as well when the television or stereo is on in a nearby room or when people are coming and going near the homework area. Oddly enough, however, children with ADD may appear freer from distraction when playing video games or watching television. This is likely due to the multisensory nature (sound, color, and constant action) of these activities. Consequently the ability to pay attention to these activities is not sufficient to rule out a diagnosis of ADD.

Has Difficulty Waiting His Turn

Many children with ADD can't wait in line as well as other youngsters of the same age. Some may try to force their way to the front of the line. Others fidget or constantly touch other children or things while waiting their turn, or they may gyrate or dance around in line.

Blurts Out Answers

Children with ADD would make ideal quiz show contestants, and they may excel at classroom drills where quick answers are rewarded. But in a structured classroom setting, these children often stand out as being impatient and uncooperative. Unable to muster the self-discipline needed to hold back an answer until they are called upon, ADD children will call out an answer as soon as they think they know it.

Moreover, in some instances, their comments may be totally unrelated to the specific class activity or discussion. This probably occurs because of the associations the child makes in response to a question. For example, the question "What is the capital of Montana?" may get the child thinking of the family trip to Montana last year, the plane landing in Helena (the capital), their horseback riding excursion at Yellowstone, and the park ranger they stopped to talk to. When the child answers, "the park ranger," there is no way for the teacher to know that the child's reply springs from having the answer, though her thoughts have speeded right past the appropriate response.

Has Difficulty Following Instructions

Children with ADD usually fare better when dealing with a single set of instructions. In fact, many become totally lost when they are given several instructions at one time. Say a parent tells a child to put on his pajamas and brush his teeth. Five minutes later, the child is wandering around aimlessly or engaged in his room playing with his toy cars, not having even begun to do what he was told. The same pattern occurs in school. When students are given numerous directions for several worksheets at a time, the child with ADD may either remember instructions for the first worksheet but not remember others, or he will remember instructions only for the last worksheet.

Consequently these children frequently appear to be out of touch with what is going on in the classroom. They also have difficulty remembering what they are supposed to do for homework, which books to take home, etc. Even if they write down assignments, the information may often be garbled or wrong.

Has Difficulty Sustaining Attention

A classic sign of ADD is the number of incomplete papers the child brings home from school. Children with ADD have difficulty completing assignments, and the appearance of their papers is usually a good indicator of the disorder. They may complete the first few problems on a page, but the remainder of the page is blank. Or their papers will look as if they rushed through the work in an attempt to get everything finished without regard to quality or correctness.

Shifts from One Uncompleted Task to Another

Parents of ADD youngsters often describe their children as having difficulty playing by themselves or as moving from one play activity to another without devoting much attention to any of them. Teachers agree. They describe students with ADD as very impulsive in learning centers and as likely to discontinue working at a project before its completion. Furthermore these children often leave remnants of their activities around their desk, the classroom, or the house.

Plays Loudly

Even when warned to calm down, children with ADD have a tough time maintaining a quiet state. They are also easily aroused by other children.

Talks Excessively

The child with ADD is often characterized as being very talkative and asking questions that are repetitive or that make little sense, " . . . like an out-of-control tape recorder that is locked on playback at a faster speed than normal," according to one parent.

Interrupts or Intrudes on Others

Parents often describe their children with ADD as interrupting them constantly when they are on the telephone or when they are talking to their spouses or friends. Efforts to make the child stop interrupting are generally futile, they say—to the point that parent-child shouting matches frequently ensue. Moreover, because of this tendency not only to interfere with what others are saying but to try and impose their will on others, children with ADD are often unpopular in group situations.

Does Not Seem to Listen

Because children with ADD have trouble focusing visually and sustaining visual attention to an individual or an activity, people often assume that the child is not listening. On the contrary, many youngsters with ADD are still able to comprehend what is going on around them. In fact, teachers and parents are often surprised that the child is able to answer questions or repeat what has been said to him. Children with severe ADD, however, may not absorb what is said.

Loses or Forgets Things

Children with more severe cases of ADD often are so poorly organized that they never seem to know where papers, pencils, articles of clothing, or other belongings were left. They often come home without the books they need for homework. They may be unable to find a shoe they just had in their hand. They also may forget to relay an important written or verbal message to their parents from their teachers—or vice versa.

Engages in Physically Dangerous Activities

Because youngsters with ADD tend to be impulsive, they often act before thinking. For instance, they might run out into a street after a ball without looking, jump from heights without consideration for potential danger, or ride a bicycle at breakneck speed without considering what is in front of them.

MORE CLUES AND CHARACTERISTICS

In addition to these symptoms, parents and teachers have found other behavioral patterns to be present in children with ADD. For example, a child often will:

Work Better One on One than Independently or in Large Groups

If your child has ADD, you may find that homework goes much more quickly if you sit with your child while he does it. Left alone to complete his homework—or classwork—the child with ADD will more than likely be up and down, fidget, daydream, and not finish the work.

Play Better with Older or Younger Children than with Same-Age Children

Children with ADD are often bossy or pick on other children. And while they may get away with bossing around younger children, same-age peers won't put up with a bossy and demanding playmate. On the other hand, older children may be more tolerant of this type of behavior. The child with ADD may control his behavior better among older children for fear of being rejected and losing the status of being able to play with them. In any case, the child is likely to be alienated from his peers and to have more relationships with younger and older children.

Have Difficulty Transferring Words from the Chalkboard to Paper

The process of transferring information requires looking, retaining in short-term memory what was seen, then unloading that information onto paper. This can be a difficult process for children with ADD, since fleeting attention limits the amount of information that can be stored in a single glance. Even when information is stored, it may be done in a faulty manner, or there will be errors (spelling mistakes, reversing information, adding or deleting information) in transferring the information from memory to paper.

Know Material Well While Studying, Then Perform Poorly on a Test

There are few situations more frustrating to parents of children with ADD than when, the night before a test, their child appears to know the material, yet the next day takes the test and scores a 42. What went wrong? During studying, the ADD child's attention is focused with the help of the parent. In testing situations, however, many more distractions are present in the classroom, and the child is on his own in staying focused and recalling information. And often he can't.

Spelling tests are frequently an exception because a teacher typically calls out a word, then waits for each child to finish writing it. For this reason, many children with ADD perform better on spelling quizzes than they do on other kinds of tests. Moreover, teachers often help children organize the way they study spelling: writing the words several times each day on Monday night, alphabetizing them on Tuesday night, using them in sentences on Wednesday night, and reviewing them on Thursday night prior to the test on Friday.

Nevertheless, once children start to daydream or become distracted in the midst of a spelling test, they have a hard time regaining their place and often leave out many words or don't complete the last parts of the test.

Respond Inconsistently to Appropriate Incentives

What often stymies parents and teachers about children with ADD is the consistency of their inconsistencies. For example, on one occasion, the child might work quickly at cleaning up his room in order to go swimming with his friends. In a similar situation at a different time, however, his parents may find him in his room playing instead of cleaning up. And if asked, "Don't you want to go swimming?" his face might light up as if to say, "Why, of course! Why would you ask such a silly question?" But he also would have to be reminded, again, about what he needs to do before he can go swimming.

Show Evidence of Poor Self-Esteem

The way a child feels about himself is reflected in the look on his face, his body language, his motivation to participate in various activities, and the things he says. Indeed many children with ADD look sad and choose not to participate in extracurricular activities. Often this is related to feelings of inadequacy and fear of more failure. More distressing to parents, however, is a child's claims that he is stupid, that nobody likes him, that he hates his parents, etc.

An analysis of these statements is complicated. The child who knows that he understands his schoolwork, but continues to make poor grades, thinks he is stupid in spite of what others tell him. This is particularly true when he sees other children getting better grades than he does, even when he is sure that he knows more than they do. Similarly, if the children he wants to play with reject him, his perception is that "nobody" likes him, even when an adult assures him that he does have close friends. From the child's perspective, it's a pretty lousy life!

Be Significantly More Active than Children of the Same Age

This characteristic identifies children with the hyperactivity component of ADD. In young children, hyperactivity may be manifested in constant movement from one place to another, only a few hours of sleep at night, restless sleep, and an inability to sit in one place for more than a few seconds. As the child gets older, hyperactivity may be characterized more by excessive fidgeting and restlessness. Furthermore older children often learn to compensate through internal controls, either as a consequence of improved neurological organization or because of increased motivation due to peer pressure or other social or tangible incentives.

Demonstrate Poor Penmanship

Penmanship is a skill that requires a plan for what one wants to write, an understanding of how to put that information on paper, and an ability to transfer that plan to paper. Many children with ADD have a great deal of difficulty mastering one or more of these steps. While formulating a plan for what they want to write, for example, they may become distracted and unable to maintain in memory the complete content of what they want to put on paper. Or they may have missed the instructions regarding how it is supposed to go down on paper. Finally, the attention to the details of putting something down on paper may be so poor that neatness is compromised. Consequently writing that may start off looking good while attention is high can quickly deteriorate as the child proceeds with the writing task. Letters may become less legible, and the spacing, size, or positioning of the letters and words may be poor. In short, the child may be able to concentrate on the neatness *or* the content, but not both simultaneously.

Lie or Make up Stories

Parents and teachers often report utter frustration with children who have ADD because they lie about obvious events. For example, the teacher may see a child take an object from another child's desk and put it in her desk. When confronted, the child denies that she took it and tends to blame someone else or shrug her shoulders. Many children with ADD will deny that they have homework, that the teacher told them about a test, that they took something from school that did not belong to them, etc. While this kind of behavior is characteristic of many young children, appropriate punishment typically causes the behavior to disappear. When the behavior persists in a child with ADD, however, it is probably related to the child's impulsiveness. In other words, a youngster with ADD will act on an idea that comes to mind without becoming conscious of it. For example, he may see a nice pencil sharpener on another child's desk and say to himself, "I sure wish I had that pencil sharpener." The next thing the child knows, it is in his hand or on his desk, and he never becomes aware of the process of taking it from the other child's desk.

It is this same lack of conscious monitoring of behavior that causes children with ADD to blurt out embarrassing and outrageous statements or to be reported for having their hands all over other children. As a consequence of ADD, the child does a poor job monitoring his own behaviors and therefore may be totally unaware of what he says or does in many instances.

WHAT'S NORMAL AND WHAT'S NOT?

You might say that many of the behaviors we have described here are exhibited by most children at one time or another. Several factors, however, distinguish youngsters with ADD from those who do not have this problem.

First, it's true that many of these behaviors are developmental in nature. In other words, they appear in children at certain ages, but youngsters typically outgrow them. In children with ADD, however, many of these behaviors persist. These youngsters either do not outgrow the behavior, or the behavior disappears for a while, then returns.

Second, children with ADD often exhibit more of these behaviors than do children without the disorder. During a normal child's early years, for example, the majority of parents deal with a few of these behaviors. But parents of children with ADD deal with far more of these behaviors and for a much longer period of time.

Finally, parents can usually control the majority of behaviors in children who do not have ADD by using behavior management strategies. Youngsters with ADD, however, tend to be resistant to most basic behavior management strategies. A harsh reprimand, for example, may be enough for most children to be convinced to straighten up. But this approach is not likely to have long-lasting effects on a child with ADD.

REDEFINING ADD

Periodically the American Psychiatric Association revises its manual that describes psychological and psychiatric conditions. This manual, which is used by professionals to help diagnose specific diseases and disorders, lists criteria that a child or adult must meet before a diagnosis can be made. The most recent edition, *Diagnostic and Statistical Manual-IV* (DSM-IV), identifies two groups of children with ADD—those who are inattentive and those who are hyperactive and impulsive.

The condition of this first group—characterized by inattentiveness—used to be called ADD without hyperactivity, or undifferentiated ADD. Now a diagnosis of ADD characterized by inattentiveness requires that at least six of the symptoms have been present for at least six months, interfere with normal functioning, and be inconsistent with the child's developmental level.

These are the symptoms for **Inattention:**

1. Often fails to give close attention to details or makes careless mistakes in schoolwork, work, or other activities

2. Often has difficulty sustaining attention in tasks or play activities

3. Often does not seem to listen to what is being said to him or her

4. Often does not follow through on instructions and fails to finish schoolwork, chores, or duties in the workplace (not due to oppositional behavior or failure to understand directions)

5. Often has difficulty organizing tasks and activities

6. Often avoids, expresses reluctance about, or has difficulty engaging in tasks that require sustained mental effort, such as schoolwork or homework

7. Often loses things necessary for tasks or activities (e.g., school assignments, pencils, books, tools, or toys)

8. Is often easily distracted by extraneous stimuli

9. Often forgetful in daily activities

What was once called ADD with hyperactivity has been renamed Hyperactivity-Impulsivity. For a diagnosis to be made, at least five of the symptoms must have been present for at least six months, interfere with normal functioning, and be inconsistent with the child's developmental level.

Here is a list of the symptoms:

Hyperactivity

1. Often fidgets with hands or feet or squirms in seat

2. Leaves seat in classroom or in other situations in which remaining seated is expected

3. Often runs about or climbs excessively in situations where it is inappropriate (in adolescents or adults, may be limited to subjective feelings of restlessness)

4. Often has difficulty playing or engaging in leisure activities quietly

5. Is always "on the go" or acts as if "driven by a motor"

6. Often talks excessively

Impulsivity

7. Often blurts out answers to questions before the questions have been completed

8. Often has difficulty waiting in lines or awaiting turn in games or group situations

9. Often interrupts or intrudes on others (e.g., butts into other's conversations or games)

In addition to the criteria mentioned for a diagnosis of ADD based on the new definition, at least some of the symptoms must have been present before seven years of age, they must appear in at least two different settings (e.g., at school and at home), they must clearly impair social and academic functioning, and they must not be due to other specified developmental or psychiatric disorders.

The symptoms listed for Inattentive ADD and for Hyperactivity-Impulsivity will be used by professionals, together with other information from physical exams, reports from teachers and observed behavior, to determine if your child has ADD. If you are a parent, it is important that you be well prepared in providing documentation of your child's behaviors, that you be able to describe his behaviors and performance in various situations, and that you consider other factors that may be causing your child to perform as he does.

COEXISTING CONDITIONS

Many children with ADD also exhibit a number of other problems. A large percentage, for instance, are persistent bed wetters, a condition called enuresis. While only about 10 percent of children in the normal population continue to wet the bed at night beyond the age of six, this problem tends to be overrepresented in the population of children with ADD. Moreover, the most common behavior approaches used to curb bed-wetting—reducing fluid intake after dinner, having the child empty his bladder before he goes to bed and again before his parents turn in—yield little consistent success in children with ADD. Even use of the bell and pad method is only moderately successful for these youngsters and may only add to the stress the child and his family are experiencing. With this method, a special pad is placed under the sheet. When it is wetted by urine, a bell connected to the pad rings. This awakens the child, who can then get up and complete urinating in the toilet. (Bell and pad kits are available at most pharmacies.)

As we have indicated earlier, many children with ADD also show signs of depression that may or may not be related to feelings of despair because of an inability to meet the child's own or others' expectations. It is painful for parents to see their children so unhappy. It is even more painful for the child to live a life characterized by feelings of helplessness and hopelessness. Careful diagnosis is necessary to determine if a child's depression has resulted from a specific event—such as a parental divorce, death of a family member, or a serious fight with a best friend, for example—or from more global factors such as continuous underachievement as a result of symptoms of ADD.

Lisa's story is a good example. Lisa is a fourth-grader who consistently makes A's and B's on her report card and who has rarely had her name put on the board for misbehaving. Lisa is also a popular child with lots of friends. For the past week or so, however, Lisa has made low D's on the majority of her tests and has failed to turn in her homework most mornings. Her name has been put on the board at least twice every day for talking back to the teacher, and on the playground she has been repeatedly reprimanded for pushing and yelling at her friends.

Lisa's teacher tried talking to her, but Lisa insisted that nothing was wrong. When the teacher threatened to call Lisa's parents, the child became defiant. "Fine," she said. "I don't care. They're not home anyway!"

When her teacher called Lisa's parents to schedule a conference, a baby-sitter reported that they were indeed out of town. Lisa's grandmother—with whom the child had been very close—had just died, and Lisa's parents had gone out of town for two weeks to attend the funeral and to help take care of Lisa's grandfather.

Once the teacher confronted Lisa about her grandmother's death, Lisa burst into tears and apologized for misbehaving and not doing her work. The school counselor spent several hours with Lisa, and within two week's time she had returned to her old self.

Many children with ADD have obsessions and compulsions as well, which might qualify for a diagnosis of Obsessive-Compulsive Disorder (OCD). Obsessions are persistent unpleasant thoughts or feelings that interfere with the ability to function normally. Compulsions are ritualistic activities in which the child must engage before moving on to another activity. For example, compulsive individuals may feel compelled to wash their hands repeatedly after touching a certain object, are driven to follow a certain pattern of behaviors prior to leaving the house, or must place objects in a particular order before feeling at ease.

Related to OCD are several other conditions often found in children with ADD. One that has received considerable media attention is Tourette's syndrome. In this and other tic disorders, the child may exhibit such behaviors as grunting; sniffing; eye blinking, scrunching, or rolling; head jerking; persistent throat clearing, etc. Many of these disorders can be treated successfully using behavioral and/or drug treatments.

The coexistence of these many disorders with ADD reinforces its neurological cause. A defect in neurotransmitter functioning has been implicated for many of these disorders and may be related, at least in part, to the inability of the brain to inhibit certain types of brain activity. For the most effective treatment plan to be designed and implemented, it is important that you discuss any unusual behaviors or concerns with your child's physician or psychologist.

2
● ● ● ● ● ● ● ● ● ● ● ● ● ● ●
Does My Child
Have ADD?

A licia, now ten, was held back a year when she
was in kindergarten. Her teacher felt that Alicia
was "immature" and would do best if she had
another year in kindergarten to mature. It was during
that first year in kindergarten that Alicia, her mother,
and her younger brother and sister moved out of their
home and into a shelter for protection from Alicia's abu-
sive father. Alicia's mother got a job at a grocery store
where her work hours required that her younger children be in a day-care center most of the day. Alicia went
to the day-care center before school and, often, after
school as well.

During Alicia's second year in kindergarten, her performance improved very little. Her teacher indicated that Alicia was refusing to do work, spent much of her time wandering around the room, and frequently bickered with other children. "I am sure she has all of the right skills," the teacher reported to Alicia's mother. "It is just so hard to get them out of her."

The mother described Alicia as very defiant and obstinate around the house—"always trying to tell me what to do," she said. The family moved into an apartment soon after Alicia's second year of kindergarten began. Alicia's mother hoped that things would settle down once her family's life became more stable. But Alicia's problems in school and at home persisted.

Now in the third grade at the age of ten, Alicia's problems still have not disappeared. Her mother recently got a better job that allows her to spend more time with the children. Still, there have been no improvements in Alicia's school performance, and her behavior at home has become even more explosive and defiant.

Maybe your child hasn't been professionally diagnosed as having ADD, but you sense that something is wrong. Or maybe she's been tested in school and been described as borderline ADD, but no treatment was recommended. Should you seek professional advice? There are questions you should ask yourself to determine if your child meets the criteria:

• Does my child daydream often and seem to be distracted easily when she is involved in an activity at home?

• Does my child have trouble sitting quietly long enough to complete her homework unless I sit with her?

• Does my child begin projects and activities but lose interest in them before they are completed?

• Does my child have difficulty following my directions?

• Does my child have difficulty sitting still at meals, for homework, in restaurants, and in church or synagogue?

• Does my child have trouble making and keeping friends who are the same age as she is?

• Is my child argumentative, and does she interrupt me constantly when I am on the telephone or talking to friends?

• Does my child seem to know school material when we study together but performs poorly on tests of the same material?

• Does my child often forget to write down her homework assignments or bring home the necessary books to complete homework or studying?

If you answered yes to many of these questions, and your child exhibits these behaviors frequently, you owe it to your child and yourself to have her evaluated either by a psychologist (preferably one who specializes in ADD) or the school system. Otherwise, if she does have ADD and her disorder is left unrecognized and untreated, the problems she is experiencing now may only become worse.

THE GREAT IMPOSTERS:
WHEN IT'S NOT ADD

Up until fifth grade, Karen breezed through school. Her grades were always well above average, and her teachers always remarked to her parents what a joy Karen was to teach. About a month into fifth grade, however, everything changed. Karen's grades began slipping, and she was often singled out in the classroom for not paying attention. She rarely turned her homework in on time and began ignoring her friends on the playground, preferring instead to play by herself. When her teacher asked Karen what was wrong, she hung her head and said, "Nothing."

Concerned, her teacher set up a conference with Karen's parents and discovered that the two had recently separated. Her parents acknowledged that they knew Karen was upset about the situation, but admitted that they'd been so busy arguing that they weren't aware of how deeply their marital problems had affected their daughter.

A number of factors can cause symptoms that mimic ADD, and these should be addressed or ruled out as causes before treating a child for the disorder:

Family Problems

Marital discord. Divorce. A family death. Substance abuse. Child abuse. These are just a few situations that can cause ADD-like behavior to surface in children. In many cases, however, youngsters bounce back once the stressful situation changes or they learn to cope with the stress. In Karen's case, for example, once her parents realized the toll their behavior was taking on their daughter, they sought family counseling to learn how best to handle their impending divorce. After several therapy sessions, Karen's behavior returned to normal. When a child's behavior is chronic, however, ADD is often the culprit.

Learning Disabilities or Other Learning or Sensory Problems

Youngsters who have difficulty seeing, hearing, or processing information may appear less interested in what people are saying or in school-related work. Those with mental handicaps, learning disabilities, or sensory deficits may also give up easily on tasks or become resigned to being "behavior problems," since structured activities with normal expectations tend to be less satisfying. For this reason, it is important to have the child's learning and sensory behaviors evaluated prior to accepting a diagnosis of ADD.

For example, when Charles, an average student, began failing in third grade, his parents scheduled a conference with his teacher. "We went over all of his papers and discovered that he was copying a lot of questions and math problems from the blackboard incorrectly. Consequently he was getting a lot of the wrong answers," his mother explains. "Most of the time, it seemed like he was copying numbers and some words and letters backward."

Charles's parents suspected that their son was just being lazy and careless, but asked the school to test him anyway. "As it turns out, Charles had a learning disability," his mother says. "Now he's enrolled in special classes, and his grades are improving."

Parenting/Caregiving Styles

The approach that parents and other caregivers use to raise and discipline a child—and the consistency among caregivers—can have a major impact on a youngster's behavior. For children with ADD, a good match with a caregiving style is particularly important.

For example, if a caregiver has an *authoritarian* style—or rules with an iron hand—the child will have few opportunities to make her own decisions. Moreover, this kind of caregiver usually takes a "spare the rod and spoil the child" approach when it comes to disciplining youngsters, which translates into punishing children (often severely) when they break any of the many rules to which they are expected to adhere.

Children with *permissive* caregivers, on the other hand, tend to have free reign to set their own rules. This kind of caregiver places few limits on the child, believing that she will learn best by pursuing her own interests and satisfying her own curiosity. What often happens instead is that permissive caregivers eventually become resigned to the fact that they have a difficult child on their hands and that few disciplinary measures seem to work. Consequently, they often give up by taking a laissez-faire approach with the child, and everyone else who must deal with the child is forced to suffer the consequences.

Finally, the *authoritative* caregiver sets clear limits but is willing to negotiate those limits in certain instances. For example, if a child's usual bedtime is 8:30 but a special show is on TV that doesn't end until 9:00, an authoritative parent might allow the child to stay up later. However, the parent also makes it clear to the child that her regular bedtime returns the next evening. Authoritative caregivers also make it a point to give their children opportunities to make decisions, as well as help them understand the consequences for making right and wrong decisions.

How do caregiving styles affect children's behavior? Research indicates that children of authoritarian and permissive caregivers tend to do more poorly in school and in life. At one extreme, children are not given the opportunity to make their own decisions; thus they may make decisions poorly when put in the position of having to structure themselves. At the other extreme is the child who has grown up in a permissive environment in which she has not had to adapt to social rules. Consequently, in a structured day-care or school environment, where there are specific expectations for her performance, she has difficulty conforming to the rules.

Consistency in caregiving styles is also important. When rules change constantly or when children are forced to deal with caregivers who have different expectations of them, they become confused and often manipulative.

Matt's story is a good example. Matt is ten years old and has a history of talking back to his parents and being defiant in school with teachers and administrators. In addition, he has had many explosive outbursts both at school and at home. Matt's parents have tried numerous behavior-management strategies over the years, ranging from verbal reprimands to yelling and spanking. None of these has worked; in fact, Matt's episodes of poor behavior have increased over time. After talking to a psychologist, Matt's parents implemented a program at home that was very rigid and structured. Under the plan, Matt lost part of his allowance and television time for each outburst and episode of talking back. The management program was begun during the summer, when there was consistent contact between Matt and his parents. Over the course of just a few weeks, both Matt and his parents acknowledged great improvement in his ability to demonstrate self-control. Initially, he became apologetic after his outbursts or episodes of talking back. Then he started catching himself in the middle of the behaviors and was able to interrupt and subdue them. Finally, he showed an overall decrease in the number of such episodes.

When Matt's parents returned to talk to the psychologist, they indicated great concerns about how both sets of grandparents were unsupportive of their efforts. The grandparents let Matt get away with talking back and excused the behaviors as Matt being "just a boy." Often they would contradict Matt's parents in front of him. His parents reported that it often took Matt several days to return to an improved level of behavior after visiting with his grandparents.

In addition to having to deal with the effects that the varying caregiving styles had on their son, Matt's parents were faced with the dilemma of either putting up with the unpleasant consequences of his behavior following a visit with his grandparents or giving the grandparents an ultimatum to change their approach or not see Matt.

Temperament

This refers to a child's innate personality, which can range from easygoing, to slow to warm up, to difficult. While temperament is determined by genetics and neurochemical makeup, some components of temperament—and, later, personality—can be modified by a child's environment. Many children who show difficult behavior patterns as infants—including colic, irregular sleep and feeding patterns, and persistent fussiness—may be easy to care for and agreeable once they grow up. On the other hand, children who are easy to care for as infants may become more difficult to handle as time passes. While a difficult temperament may affect aspects of the child's behavior and learning, it does not always predict ADD. It is important to differentiate between specific characteristics of ADD and those of a difficult temperament before establishing a treatment plan.

Fatigue, Illness, and Hunger

Behavior changes are common when any of us feels tired, hungry, or ill, and this is particularly true for children. Those with greater needs for sleep or those who tend to have irregular eating habits may be tired or hungry more often during the day, and often changes in their behavior are simply a consequence of these factors. For example, the first-grader who becomes wild and uncontrollable periodically may be having a difficult time coping without the nap she was used to taking at home or in kindergarten last year. The cumulative effect of sleep deprivation can cause problems as well.

Youngsters who are prone to middle-ear infections, constipation, or similar chronic problems may also show alterations in behavior as a result of their discomfort. Therefore it is important to consider life patterns and chronic illnesses as possible causes of behavior before considering a diagnosis of ADD.

Diet

While changes in behavior have been reported for many children in response to certain diet products and foods (e.g., sweets), researchers have found little evidence to support this claim. And there is scant evidence that allergies to other environmental substances may alter a child's behavior. Unfortunately many unfounded claims and theories have received a great deal of national publicity on television talk shows and in tabloids. As a result, viewers are often led to believe that there is sound scientific evidence to support these claims. In fact, there is none.

Nevertheless the wealth of anecdotal reports of children whose behavior has improved dramatically with the elimination of certain foods makes diet an important consideration for children with behavior and learning problems. Thus parents should begin by observing the child's short-term behavior following eating or drinking certain substances. In addition, they might try decreasing, one at a time, the common allergenic products in the child's diet that the child consumes in large quantities—examples are chocolate, tomato products, eggs, and milk.

If a child has a history of allergies or is congested at certain times during the year, your physician may recommend allergy testing. However, in general, although allergic responses to foods or environmental substances may make an attention problem worse, they are rarely the cause of the problem.

Teacher-Child Mismatch

Unfortunately, there are rare times when a teacher's style clashes with a child's temperament and learning style. And sometimes neither adjustment by the teacher nor adaptation by the child can solve the problem. Of course, not every teacher your child has will be outstanding. Nevertheless, parents hope that their children will be resilient enough to accommodate an undesirable teacher's personality and teaching style. But not all children have this resilience. In fact, some teachers may be so difficult for a child to accommodate to that the stress of this daily confrontation may elicit somatic complaints (e.g., headaches and stomach aches) from the child, as well as symptoms that mimic ADD.

What can parents do in such situations? Most schools have an informal policy of not changing a child's class once school starts. But by taking an assertive approach to the problem, you may be able to convince school administrators to bend the rules. Keep in mind, though, that school administrators must deal with many children's needs, and that a request for a change of teachers should be made only for sound educational reasons, and after other approaches have failed.

So before you begin your campaign, gather documentation to prove that your child has a history of good performance in school and is capable of doing the work, but is so distressed by the teacher's approach that her work productivity has suffered. Make an appointment to present your argument and documentation to the school administrator. If she refuses to consider your request, let her know that you intend to call or show up in person with any and all new information about your child's problems in school until the move is made! Be pleasant and cordial, but also firm and persistent. Your child's present and future success may be at stake, and that is something worth fighting for.

As a parent of a child with ADD, it is critical that you play the role of advocate. You can best do this by educating yourself and others about this common disorder, by doing whatever you can to minimize the stresses your child experiences, and by helping others who interact with your child regularly to do the same.

TO TEST OR NOT TO TEST

When children have behavior or learning problems, parents are often advised by a number of sources to have their youngsters tested for academic and psychological strengths and weaknesses. With a preschool child, the testing must generally be conducted by a private psychologist. For a school-age child, parents have the option of having the school system test the child or having tests administered privately. Schools are reluctant to test children unless there is significant evidence of learning problems. Procedures for testing through the school system are time-consuming and involve wading through many complex bureaucratic steps, both prior to testing and for follow-up information. Nevertheless, if your child is having problems and you want to find out what's wrong, don't let these drawbacks dissuade you.

In fact, federal education laws require school systems to test any child who is three years of age or older who might be eligible for special education services.

Psychological and academic testing can be particularly useful for several types of children. First, it may benefit those who show particular strengths *and* particular weaknesses in their academic work. In other words, when a child performs above average in some areas of academics but does very poorly in others, this may indicate a learning disability that may either accompany ADD or be a consequence of poor attention during the early years.

Second, testing can be useful for children who show generalized delays in all academic areas. Again, this developmental delay may accompany ADD or be a consequence of it. Nevertheless, if the delays are significant enough, the child may be eligible for additional remedial education programs through the schools.

Finally, testing may be useful in pinpointing a significant social or emotional problem demonstrated in the educational setting. In this case, projective testing and various types of rating scales are used to identify the type of, and sometimes the reason for, the social and emotional problems.

Formal psychological testing of children is a lengthy process that may involve several hours of contact between the psychologist and the child, often over the course of several days. Testing generally involves measures of intelligence (common tests in this area include the Wechsler Intelligence Scale for Children, the Stanford-Binet Intelligence Test, and the Kaufman Assessment Battery for Children), measures of academic achievement (the Peabody Individual Achievement Test, the Kaufman Test of Educational Achievement, the Woodcock-Johnson Tests of

Achievement, and the Wechsler Individual Achievement Test are most common), and may involve measures of emotional status, specific language skills, and perceptual-motor skills.

SCHOOL SERVICES AVAILABLE AND YOUR RIGHTS AS A PARENT

In most cases, a recommendation to have a child tested through a school program is made by the Student Support Team (see page 147)—and only after trying numerous other approaches to help the child in the educational setting. As a parent, you must give written consent for the testing. You also have a right to review the results of all testing that is done.

If you agree to have your child tested, don't do anything or treat him any differently to prepare him for the procedure. In other words, don't put him to bed earlier than usual. Also avoid prompting him or giving him medication he would not normally take. You want the psychologist to see your child in his typical state—demonstrating performances and exhibiting behaviors that are representative of how he normally performs and behaves in the classroom. Except, of course, that testing is generally done on a one-on-one basis.

Following the testing, you will be invited in for a conference to discuss various options based on your child's test results. If test results indicate that your child qualifies for special education services, you will have the opportunity to learn about and consider the type and extent of services he needs. Keep in mind that special education services for eligible children are based on what a child *needs* rather than what services are currently being provided by the school. Therefore, if there is evidence of a severe problem, more intensive intervention should be prescribed.

Most schools use the principle of Least Restrictive Environment, which supports the idea that children with special needs should be served in a setting that is as close to normal as possible, while simultaneously meeting their educational needs. If the school recommends special education services for your child—or if you feel that special services are needed but the school does not make those recommendations—you have numerous rights for due process to question or appeal the school's decision. To keep this process as productive and cordial as possible, however, it is often wise to discuss your options with a professional or another knowledgeable parent who will serve as your and your child's advocate.

There will be decisions to make every step of the way. First, you'll need to decide whether or not to have your child tested. Second, if he is tested, you must decide if you feel the test results accurately reflect your child's ability. If not, what recourse do you have? Then you need to decide whether or not to accept special education placement if your child is eligible. If he is not eligible for special services, you must decide whether to accept the decision or to appeal it. If he is eligible, you must decide, together with school personnel, on the best placement for your child. There are a range of options here: part-time placement in a resource class, full-time placement in a special education class, placement in a special facility for children with the type of problem your child is experiencing, and so on. Finally, you'll need to decide on specific goals and objectives that the program should strive to achieve with your child.

Decisions, decisions. If you find yourself feeling confused, overwhelmed, and fearful of making the wrong choices, find a knowledgeable friend, a professional, or a member of your local ADD support group (see Appendix) to assist you with these important decisions.

After frustrating encounters with school personnel to get what they think their child needs, some parents begin thinking about soliciting private help. Some, for example, may opt to have their child tested privately by a licensed clinical psychologist or school psychologist at their own expense. Schools will often accept these testing results in making eligibility and placement decisions about the child.

Some parents consider home-schooling their youngsters. Granted, home-schooling may provide more opportunities for the child to feel successful, offer a more distraction-free environment, and provide the one-on-one teaching by which he is likely to learn best, but it may also be counterproductive. Unless there are also opportunities built into the child's schedule for social and recreational activities with peers, his learning may lack in several dimensions. Moreover, if interactions between the parent and the child have tended to be unpleasant, home-schooling can easily increase both the parent's and the child's levels of frustration.

Other parents consider transferring their child to private school. Youngsters with ADD often improve in private-school settings because of smaller class sizes and greater opportunities for one-on-one interactions with their teachers. But this option is almost always an expensive one that many parents simply cannot afford.

PUBLIC SCHOOL ALTERNATIVES

Unfortunately, based on current guidelines, children with ADD often do not qualify for special education services, despite the fact that their test results or classroom performance demonstrate the presence of mild academic problems or social and emotional problems. If this is your dilemma, request that other recommendations be made to help your child overcome these problems. For instance, additional behavioral interventions may be used. Medication may also be considered, if it has not been tried in the past. Chapter I remedial education services might be available for youngsters experiencing difficulties in reading or math. ("Chapter I" refers to the section of a federal education law that describes remedial teaching programs in math and reading in most public schools for children with academic problems.) Special volunteer tutors at all educational levels may also be used to help the child in areas of weakness or to provide a mentor to help the child through difficult emotional and behavioral episodes.

Children with ADD who continue to have problems in school that interfere with their learning are eligible for special services even if they do not meet the criteria for any special education program. *Under Section 504 of the Rehabilitation Act, children with ADD have a right to special modifications within the school to assist them to be more successful.* This may include testing on an individual basis, the use of a tape recorder or typewriter, special tutors, and various other strategies.

When schools provide special services to children and demonstrate their commitment to helping your child learn as best he can, it is important that you express your appreciation for the extra help of school personnel.

On the flip side, when school personnel appear unresponsive or insensitive to the needs of your child, you should exercise your rights to call conferences or hearings, or use legal means, if necessary, to make your child's educational experiences as positive and productive as possible. Before you play the role of militant against the school system, however, be sure that you can describe the efforts you have made at home to help your child be more successful. That way, your requests of the school system are viewed as reasonable in sharing the educational responsibilities for your child.

A parent's log, such as the one presented on pages 48–51, is the best way to provide evidence of your efforts both to help your child and to work with the school. While this log need not be extensive, it should reflect the types of behaviors you typically observe and respond to in your child in nonschool settings. It should also document the various strategies you have used and your child's response to them, as well as any contacts you have had with professionals both inside and outside the school.

A PARENT'S LOG

4/7 (Saturday)
Chad woke up whining. No TV until he was dressed and finished breakfast. Wandered around the house, sitting down only briefly to take a few spoonfuls of cereal. After one hour, I walked him through everything, but he got no TV for the A.M. After this ordeal, I told him he had to have his room cleaned up before he went outside. Twenty minutes later he was in his room playing. Reminded him every ten minutes. Lunchtime and room still not cleaned. Took kids to run errands. Offered to eat out if kids behaved during ride. Chad couldn't keep his hands to himself. Was all over the store. Reminders about eating out helped for no more than a minute or so. We went back home as fast as possible. (I hated that the other kids did well and couldn't get to eat out.) Chad spent P.M. in his room until he thought he could control himself. Tried a few times, but wound up back in his room. Came out for dinner and seemed to try hard but squirmed, giggled, and half sat, half stood while he ate. Baths, stories, and bedtime. Lots of "curtain calls" for Chad and eventually he stayed in his room and went to sleep. The poor kid got to do nothing all day. Poor all of us!

4/8 (Sunday)
Why do we all keep trying to do the church thing? Jack
had to take Chad out after he squirmed his way along
two pews and hummed through most of the sermon. We
all went out to eat afterward. The three kids ate on the
run so that they could play on the playground
equipment. The P.M. was a disaster again. Friends came
over and Chad interrupted lots and wanted to be the
center of attention. I talked to him in his room, and
eventually Jack sent him to Time Out (see page 91). The
friends stayed for dinner. Chad was noisy, but we tried
to keep him busy helping out. As long as we kept him
occupied, he did fine. Bedtime, etc., a repeat of
yesterday.

4/9 (Monday)
No TV until dressed and fed. Didn't get TV. Had to
walk him through dressing while sister waited for us to
head out the door for school. Two "sad faces" from
teacher today and scribbling in the homework pad.
Looked through bookbag and found spelling test. (40!
He knew the words perfectly when we studied.) Called a
friend for homework assignment. While Jackie did her
homework and Aaron played with building blocks, I sat
with Chad for one hour to do 15 minutes worth of
homework. Let him go outside. Came in 30 minutes
later crying. He had a fight with his "friends" and they
didn't want to play with him. He stayed in and watched
a video. Tried to sit down and read with kids. Chad was
up and down and rolling around. Off to his room again.

P.M. routine a little better. Probably tired from school, etc.

4/10 (Tuesday)
Same wearying A.M. routine. Kids almost missed their ride. Bookbag got "lost" on the way home from school. Finally tracked it down, but not much in it. Two days worth of incomplete papers and scribbling in homework pad again. Called friend again for homework assignment. Teacher is supposed to be signing pad but has not done it for past several weeks. It seemed to be helping. I have meeting with teacher tomorrow. Chad looked tired today. Gave "no outside or TV" options if homework was not completed in 45 minutes. Barely made it for 20 minutes worth of homework. Went outside for a while and came in. Was really noisy and picking on Aaron a lot. But we made it through another day.

4/11 (Wednesday)
Met with Chad's teacher this A.M. She acknowledged that she has not been signing his homework pad consistently. She said she is overwhelmed with many kids in class who need individual attention, particularly late in the day. She said she knows Chad has lots of ability, but she can't quite figure out how to tap it. She has tried moving his seat several times, having him sit next to an ambitious student who would help him, given him jobs to do, etc. Nothing has worked for her. Sounds like what we have been dealing with at home, but she has to deal with a lot more kids. We finally decided on

requesting a Student Support Team meeting to get some more heads together to figure out what we can do. I am going to give Cindy down the street a call for some tips, since she went through this whole thing with Gretchen last year.

3

• • • • • • • • • • • • • • • • • •

ADD:
Causes and Effects

*D*avid, a sixth-grader, is an adopted child who has always struggled academically. Since kindergarten his teachers have described him as easily distracted and as having a short attention span. But, they add, he is usually a very sociable and pleasant child.

This year, David had detention numerous times, primarily for coming to class unprepared and for wandering the halls without a pass. And recently he was suspended for two days after getting into a fistfight with another child.

At home, David's parents say he rarely appears motivated to do schoolwork and that he never lets them *know when he has homework or exams. Because of this lack of communication, his parents claim they are unable to monitor their son's progress or help him prepare for tests.*

David spends most of his time at home listening to music and reading. Despite his academic and behavioral problems, he says he likes school. Nonetheless David appears headed on a course that can only lead to increasing problems both at school and at home.

CAUSES

Whose Fault Is It?

Whenever children have problems, there's a natural tendency to look for something or someone to blame for their misfortune. In David's case, one might point the finger at his parents, arguing that they appear too permissive. After all, what "good" parents rely on a child to tell them when he has a test or when an important assignment is due? If a child is failing, wouldn't it make more sense for the parents to check with the child's teacher about his assignments? Furthermore, when a youngster is sent to detention as often as David has been, and suspended for fighting as well, doesn't this suggest a lack of discipline on the home front?

On the other hand, David is adopted. And since ADD is known to have biological roots, perhaps he has inherited the disorder from one of his biological parents.

Then again, maybe David's teachers are partly to blame. After all, he appears to have been labeled as impulsive and easily distracted since kindergarten. And since children can usually sense how others—particularly adults—perceive them, they often develop self-concepts to meet the lowered expectations others have of them. If this is true in David's case, he is likely caught in a vicious cycle. Because his teachers perceive him as a low achiever and a behavior problem, he has little self-esteem. This, in turn, can easily lead to poor social-adjustment skills, developmental delays, and academic failure.

The Most Likely Culprit

ADD can leave everyone involved feeling frustrated. The child performs poorly even when he is motivated and putting forth his best effort. Parents feel incompetent because the child is not responding to their attempts at consistent behavior management and child-rearing approaches. Teachers feel frustrated and inadequate because all of the approaches they learned in school and at workshops have proven unsuccessful at getting one particular child to perform to his potential.

All of this paints a bleak picture—one in which everyone involved feels despondent, unsatisfied, and even responsible for the dilemma. But the truth is that no one individual is to blame for the child's problems, although the behavior patterns of parents, teachers, and the child himself can certainly aggravate the situation. Research indicates, however, that the major source of the ADD child's dramatic social and academic problems is biological.

In fact, recent research has pinpointed specific differences in the way the brain functions in individuals with ADD as compared to those who do not have the disorder. This research has used a procedure called positron emission tomography (PET), which provides a dynamic picture of the brain and shows the levels of activity in various parts of the brain at specific times. When a person is reading, for example, the visual cortex—the part of the brain responsible for interpreting visual material—appears most active on the PET, while other areas of the brain appear less active. Similarly, when a person is listening to music with his eyes closed, the auditory cortex appears very active, while other areas appear less active.

The PET scan procedure has been used for research purposes to identify brain differences in individuals with many types of suspected brain disorders. To date, it has revealed differences between normal individuals and those with depression, schizophrenia, Alzheimer's disease, Obsessive-Compulsive Disorder, and others.

What differences does the PET scan reveal in the brains of children with ADD versus those without the disorder? One apparent difference has surfaced in the frontal lobe, an area of the brain responsible for receiving incoming information and deciphering which information is important and which is not. The brain performs this function in a way that we are unaware of. For example, you may sleep through a truck rumbling by your house in the middle of the night but awaken immediately when you hear the quiet whimpering of your child down the hall. What appears to happen is that this part of the brain has decided that the sound of the truck is unimportant and can be ignored. Consequently no action is taken and other parts of the brain remain dormant. In the case of your whimpering child, however, the brain has decided that this information is important. As a result, the part of the brain that processes auditory information is awakened, together with the other parts of the brain that make you open your eyes and come awake.

In a classroom setting, when this area of the frontal lobe is functioning normally, a child can easily pay attention to the teacher, concentrate on the work in front of him, or focus on the announcement he hears over the loudspeaker. However, when this part of the brain is not functioning well, all incoming information tends to compete on an equal basis. A nearby child shuffling papers at his seat. A truck rumbling by outside the window. The smells of lunch being prepared down the hall. A reading group reading aloud in the corner of the room. In the ADD child, all of these scenarios receive the same attention by the brain as what the child is trying to focus on.

Furthermore, this "executive" part of the brain also appears to inhibit activity in parts of the brain that are unnecessary for certain tasks. It limits activity in the motor (movement) area of the brain when it is desirable to remain still for a task. When the frontal lobe area is not doing its job correctly, no such controls on movement may occur, and the child may appear fidgety and hyperactive.

PET scan studies indicate that the frontal lobe operates more sluggishly in individuals with ADD. The reason for this probably relates to how certain chemicals called neurotransmitters do their job in this part of the brain. The brain is composed of billions of nerve cells. For messages to be communicated from one part of the brain to another, nerve impulses travel along the nerve cells and then to adjoining nerve cells across a space called a synapse, the gap between nerve cells. For nerve impulses to move across the gaps efficiently there must be one or more chemicals, called neurotransmitters, in the space. These chemicals are produced at the end of the nerve cells. Neurotransmitters are continually being produced, secreted into the synapse, and reabsorbed by the nerve cells as nerve impulses continue to move from one part of the brain to another. In children with ADD, however, it appears that while neurotransmitters are produced normally, they are reabsorbed back into the nerve cells too quickly for impulses to travel across the synapse efficiently.

The result? A disorganized pattern of attention and arousal, often inefficient processing of information in various parts of the brain responsible for handling visual and auditory information, problems retrieving information from memory, and, in some cases, uncontrolled and disorganized movement patterns.

The implications of this problem with the brain can be profound. Aside from making decisions about what incoming information is important and should be paid attention to versus what information would best be ignored, the frontal lobe also decides what other parts of the brain should be activated and inhibited to efficiently process important incoming information. For example, if a child is taking a test, the visual cortex of the brain and areas of memory storage are most likely to be activated. At the same time, the frontal lobe would inhibit activity in the auditory cortex so that the child would not be distracted by noises around him during the test. In individuals with ADD, this efficient process does not occur. Therefore parts of the brain that should be inhibited, such as the motor area, may not be. The result: a child who fidgets and changes position often during an activity when he should be sitting still.

In the broader picture, the inability of the child's co-ordinating center of the brain to control thinking and moving processes causes him to be inconsistent, impulsive, and out of control. It is these factors that create the severe level of frustration that everyone in the child's environment—and the child himself—experiences.

Here's a good analogy to help you empathize with your ADD child. Imagine trying to carry on a conversation with someone at a loud party or in a noisy restaurant. It can be difficult to hear the person you're talking to because, while you're trying to listen to her, you are being bombarded with other sights and sounds that are competing on an equal basis. So you strain and struggle to focus on what is being said but are often unsuccessful.

What's happening here is that the brain is trying to

sort out the important sounds from all the other competing sounds, but it is having a difficult time doing so. Essentially, all of the stimuli in your environment are competing for your attention on the same level, and your brain is failing in its task to help you sort out the important information.

ADD children's lives appear to follow this pattern. The assignment on the board that must be copied down is competing for attention with a conglomeration of other sights and sounds, as well as other thoughts that are racing through the child's head. As a result, the child has difficulty following instructions, completing assignments, controlling unnecessary movements, retrieving information for tests and discussions, and processing other information appropriately.

We do not know why children with ADD can efficiently concentrate at certain times but not at others. We do know, however, that the inconsistencies and general patterns of difficulty are frustrating for the children as well as for everyone else around them. Indeed, these dysfunctions not only interfere with the child's ability to read, write, and solve mathematical problems, but also with his ability to get along with his peers and family members.

The Thyroid Connection

Recently scientists discovered the first link between a genetic defect and Attention Deficit Disorder. Researchers at the National Institutes of Diabetes and Digestive and Kidney Diseases in Bethesda, Maryland, found that children suffering from a rare genetic disease—resistance to thyroid hormone—also show a very high rate of Attention Deficit Disorders. When a specific gene works correctly, a particular protein in the body responds to thyroid hormone and helps control metabolism, heart rate, and, in the fetus, brain development. However, when the gene is defective, the protein performs abnormally. This may result in short stature, enlargement of the thyroid gland, cardiac problems, and ADD. About 70 percent of the children and half of the adults with thyroid hormone resistance showed symptoms of ADD.

This discovery will likely play a role in early identification of individuals with thyroid hormone resistance, who then stand a good chance of developing ADD. Unfortunately, it is unlikely that this discovery will lead to any cure for ADD in the near future, either for the very small percentage of the population with thyroid hormone resistance or for other individuals who show symptoms of Attention Deficit Disorders. Nevertheless, this finding provides reinforcing evidence that ADD is neurologically based. It also provides hope that other causes for Attention Deficit Disorders will be discovered in the near future.

EFFECTS

The ADD Child at Home

Most children with ADD are identified as having the disorder because of difficulties they are experiencing in school. Yet, in many instances—and often long before a diagnosis is made—parents harbor suspicions that their child is different from their other children or from youngsters of the same age.

Eight-year-old Pete's parents, for example, say that calm moments shared with their son have been few and far between. Typically, when told to do something, Pete's responses have been unpredictable—with even simple requests frequently resulting in conflict. From an early age, Pete has habitually gotten into everything, touching breakable items on shelves and taking things out of cabinets, drawers, and the refrigerator without asking. His parents have been reluctant to take Pete out in public and even felt anxious about inviting friends and family to their homes, for fear that Pete would misbehave.

At school, teachers have repeatedly reported that Pete's work has not been up to par and that he has trouble getting along with his peers. When Pete complains that he's dumb and that nobody likes him, his parents try to reassure him. They recognize that he's upset and frustrated. But sometimes it's difficult for his parents to get past their own feelings of anguish and frustration.

It takes enormous skill and patience for parents of a child with ADD to maintain a positive outlook on the family dynamics. In fact, the best way for Pete's parents to achieve this goal is to picture the disorder from their son's perspective. His name is called out sternly and repeatedly—to do something, to stop doing something, to pay attention, etc. All too often, he feels well prepared for a test but for some reason does poorly. He longs to take part in group activities at school or in the neighborhood, but no one wants him to be part of their group. And no matter how hard he tries to stay in his seat while doing schoolwork, Pete's teacher is constantly yelling at him to stay seated and remain still.

The behavior patterns of children with ADD vary from one individual to the next, whether at home, in school, or in other settings. At home, children with ADD generally prefer watching television, playing video games, or playing outside. Many have trouble playing independently; thus, when not involved in these preferred activities, they tend to follow a parent around or move from one unsatisfying activity to another. This kind of behavior is likely to frustrate the parent, who in turn is likely to lash out in anger or make unrealistic demands on the child.

The child with ADD shares his parent's frustrations. Moreover, when he's yelled at frequently and loses privileges more often than his siblings do, the effect on his self-esteem can be dramatic. Unfortunately this, of course, can further frustrate his parents and leave them feeling guilty and incompetent.

The ADD child's day is also filled with crisis points. Faced with the task of meeting a parent's demands, completing a chore, or making a decision, conflict within himself or with someone else in his environment is generally inevitable. Granted, these crisis points exist with other children as well, but they are far more exaggerated when a child with ADD is involved.

The list below summarizes these major home crisis points.

Getting out of bed
Getting dressed
Eating breakfast
Gathering necessary materials/supplies for school
Dressing for outdoors
Leaving the house
Waiting for the bus
Changing into after-school clothes
Relating events of the school day to parents
Reviewing daily work
Doing homework
Preparing bookbag for next day
Playing indoors or outdoors
Coming in from outdoors
Eating dinner
Bathing or showering
Preparing for bed
Going to bed

In the next chapter, we offer a home program for parents and their children with ADD on how to get through these crisis points as smoothly as possible.

The ADD Child at School

ADD is frequently misunderstood by teachers and school administrators. Children with the disorder are often labeled troublemakers or slow learners, and their parents are implored to use stronger disciplinary measures or to spend more time with their children studying and doing homework.

This overly simplistic approach only reinforces parents' feelings of guilt and frustration. In most instances, they have already tried a variety of strategies to help their child be more successful at school.

The child with ADD feels equally frustrated and discouraged. He's aware that his name is put on the board more often than are other children's. He knows his grades are not as good as they should be, considering his knowledge of the material. He also recognizes that his peers don't like playing with him because he's impulsive and bossy.

In other words, he feels trapped in a no-win situation. His teacher is on his back at school; his parents are on his back at home. Yet he may very well be trying as hard as he possibly can to be successful and to meet others' expectations of him.

A wise teacher will recognize that if three or four days of missed recess fail to modify the child's behavior, then the strategy is ineffective. She will then look for other approaches to help improve the child's work habits and behavior in the classroom. After all, a child who is continuously punished at school for lack of performance or inappropriate behavior—and is then punished at home for the same reasons—will eventually shut down and show little motivation at all to improve.

The ADD Child in the Community

Children with ADD often show little interest in participating in extracurricular activities that involve groups or teams. The reasons for this stem from their inability to control their impulsiveness, to wait their turn, and to stay focused on such activities. In ball games, for example, the child with ADD is more likely to be walking the fence, gazing at an airplane flying overhead, or pulling up grass than concentrating on the game.

However, these children often find success in individualized extracurricular activities. In martial arts or dance, for example, where there is more give and take between the child and an instructor, children with ADD have an easier time paying attention. These kinds of activities are also less competitive, thus allowing the child more opportunities to experience and enjoy individual success.

The most important thing for parents, teachers, and members of the community to recognize about ADD is that it's an organic problem not unlike asthma, diabetes, or a chronic aching back. Those afflicted with these ailments are victims, just as children are who have ADD. And while there may be no cures, there are remedies or treatments for these problems, just as there are for ADD.

But in the case of ADD, the help and understanding of others is required to provide those remedies. Few children prefer punishment and loss of privileges over rewards and positive attention. Therefore it is crucial to

view the child with ADD as a victim who longs to perform better, but who simply needs help to do so. This is
the central idea of the home program in the next chapter
and of Chapter 6, on the role of teachers.

4

● ● ● ● ● ● ● ● ● ● ● ● ● ● ● ● ● ● ●

A Home Program for Children with ADD

*A*s a second-grader, Margaret made straight A's and B's and was in the gifted program. Since entering the third grade, however, her grades have been slipping. Her teachers report that she does not pay attention in class and that much of her work is incomplete. During work time in the classroom, Margaret is often caught daydreaming or fidgeting with her pencil. She daydreams during class discussions as well but always seems to have the right answer when called upon.

At home, Margaret's parents claim that she procrastinates too much. "She'll spend over an hour doing thirty minutes of homework—unless we provide direct supervision while she is working," says her mother. "And if we walk away, Margaret's mind appears to wander, or she starts fidgeting and gets nothing accomplished."

Margaret likes to draw and read, but her favorite activity is playing Nintendo. And while she is able to sit calmly at the dinner table, she has to be repeatedly told to eat.

Lately Margaret has been complaining to her parents that she's stupid and that nobody likes her. In response, they mention her previous good grades and try to point out how many birthday parties she's recently been invited to attend. Still, Margaret's parents are concerned about her slipping grades. They also worry that she may be suspended from the gifted program. Above all, they are frustrated because they know how intelligent their daughter is. They watch her complete her assignments perfectly when they sit down with her at night. They are thrilled when they quiz her and she answers nearly all of their questions correctly. What they cannot understand is why, when she gets to school, she appears both unable to complete her work and to remember what she's learned the night before.

When they discuss their concerns with Margaret's teacher, she assures them that it's "probably just a stage" Margaret is going through. But Margaret's parents don't believe that and make an appointment for their daughter to be evaluated by a child psychologist.

The psychologist spends about thirty minutes with Margaret's parents gathering family, medical, and educational history. This helps to pinpoint potential environmental and medical causes for the symptoms Margaret's parents describe. It also points out patterns of behavior over time. For example, Margaret did well in the unstructured setting of preschool and kindergarten but began having problems in later years, when there were more formal rules for her to follow. The psychologist asks how Margaret behaves in other settings and around different kinds of people.

The psychologist requests copies of all of Margaret's report cards to date. A review of report cards is important in clarifying her academic history and changes over time. In addition, the comments teachers have made on Margaret's report cards can also reveal classroom behaviors in different grades.

The psychologist asks to look at standardized test score results and samples of Margaret's schoolwork. Finally, he spends time with Margaret discussing her hobbies and interests and who her friends are—trying to get a good general picture of who Margaret is and how she feels about herself.

Margaret's parents make a second appointment for formal testing, including intelligence and achievement tests, projective tests to evaluate personality characteristics, and measures of depression and anxiety. In addition, Margaret's parents are given a checklist to complete based on Margaret's behavior at home. Margaret's teacher is also asked to fill out a checklist regarding behaviors she has noticed in the classroom.

When the evaluation process is complete and all of the data are analyzed, the psychologist calls Margaret's parents in for a consultation. Diagnosis: ADD. Margaret's parents are not surprised, but they do have numer-

ous questions to ask the psychologist about how to work with Margaret's teachers, how to tell her siblings about Margaret's disorder, and what strategies they should use to handle Margaret herself.

PARENTS AS ADVOCATES

Nobody knows a child better than her parents. That's why your role in treating your child with ADD is so important. Not only must you be well versed about your child's disorder, you must use your knowledge to see that others who care for your child also have a good understanding of what ADD is—and isn't. Moreover, you must take whatever steps are necessary to assure that your child's special needs are being met both inside and outside the home.

It's not an easy job. Caring for a child who has ADD can be extremely frustrating. At times you will feel helpless and wonder, "Why me?" But you will also feel hopeful in knowing that you *can* make a difference in your child's life. As she grows and matures, you *will* notice improvement. And you can take credit for the critical role you played in helping your child be the best she can be.

The first step in becoming an advocate for your ADD child is to learn all you can about her disorder. Reading this book is an excellent start. You may also want to look at other books on the subject; our list of recommended readings should help get you started. Popular magazines often have articles devoted to ADD. Clip any you run across and maintain a file for your information. Also ask your child's doctor to pass along any journal articles she thinks you might find worthwhile. We have included a list of selected books, pamphlets, and videotapes on ADD in this book's Appendix.

Once you have a good working knowledge of ADD, your next goal is to find ways to minimize your child's weaknesses and maximize her strengths. You can do this by following these general guidelines, designed to help you set your child up for success both at home and at school.

SETTING YOUR CHILD UP FOR SUCCESS AT HOME: GENERAL APPROACHES

• *Give your child a simple but straightforward explanation of what ADD is and help her to understand how the disorder affects her.* If you have trouble finding the right words to explain ADD, there are several good children's books you can read to your child or give to her to read (see Appendix). If your youngster is old enough to read one of these books alone, however, be sure to discuss the material she's read and answer all of her questions afterward.

It's a good idea to have other siblings read or listen to the material and participate in discussions as well. They can serve as allies and supporters for the child's efforts. If they have a clear understanding of ADD, they will also be less likely to make fun of efforts that fall short of success.

• *Explain your child's problem to other family members as well.* Then point out and explain why sometimes her behavior must be treated differently from theirs.

• *Make a list of family rules and review them with all of your children*. Make sure each one is understood, then post them on the refrigerator as a reminder. Rules should be established following conflicts and dilemmas. For example, if your children getting up from the table repeatedly during meals interferes with your desire to have everyone sit at the table together to eat, you might introduce a rule such as Rule 5 in the example below, about asking to be excused before leaving the table. Rules can be introduced to family members by saying, "Maybe we should have a rule for that," or "Why don't we think of a rule we can set up to help us with this problem?" Your children can often be involved in helping to establish the rules, and the rules can be discussed before they are implemented.

FAMILY RULES

1. We pick up after ourselves.
2. We talk politely to one another.
3. We do our chores every day.
4. We don't interrupt.
5. We ask to be excused before leaving the table.
6. We do our work before we play.
7. We let someone know where we are at all times.

• *Assign your youngster with ADD chores she can handle easily, and set up a reward system for completing each task*. For example, you might place stickers or stars on a chart and agree that a completely filled row can be cashed in for a special treat. When first using this approach, lesser rewards may be given for having fewer stickers.

• *Gradually add more difficult chores to a child's list as she masters the easier ones.* This will help her develop a sense of responsibility. Also, if she is challenged and prevails, her self-esteem will soar. On the other hand, if she fails, the number and difficulty of chores should be reduced to a level where success is more probable.

• *Whenever possible, let your child with ADD set her own personal goals, then work at her own pace achieving them.* That way she can experience the joy of accomplishing something on her own.

• *Once goals are set, work up parent-child contracts.* Discuss each goal, then write and sign a contract with each of you outlining what action you plan to take to see that the goal is met. Suppose your child's goal is to clean her room twice a week. She would write, "I will clean my room twice a week," then sign her name. Next you would write a similar statement below hers—something like "I will help her reach this goal by reminding her of it on Thursdays and Sundays. When she has cleaned her room as promised for two consecutive weeks, we will go see a movie together." Should this approach not work for several consecutive weeks, it might be necessary to return to looking at shorter-term goals which can be rewarded more immediately.

• *Make sure the expectations you have of your child with ADD are realistic and that the consequences for poor or no performance are realistic.* Let's return to the case of Margaret, described at the beginning of this chapter. Expecting that she will be able to finish her homework in a short period of time, and unsupervised, or that she will receive all A's on her report card is setting Margaret up for failure. Similarly, depriving Margaret of her favorite activities—like drawing, reading, and Nintendo—because of lack of success only leads to a more frustrated child and strips her of the few things she consistently does well and enjoys. Expectations should be such that children are able to attain success often enough to earn positive consequences and feel good about their accomplishments.

• *Point out how the child's actions affect what happens around her.* She might, for example, start hitting the dog for tearing up her favorite doll—the one you told her to put away numerous times in the past thirty minutes. Children can start becoming accountable for the consequences of their actions when you review with them how what they do (or don't do) affects what happens afterward.

• *Help your child find an activity in which she can excel.* Children with ADD often suffer from poor self-esteem and constantly think, "I'm no good." This is particularly true for children with siblings who shine at certain activities. To boost your child's self-esteem, help her find activities in which she, too, can shine. Look for unique activities, however, ones in which she cannot easily be compared to other family members or to her circle of friends, as well as ones that do not involve groups of youngsters competing against one another. These might include such activities as knitting, putting puzzles together, playing an unusual musical instrument (like the oboe), or the martial arts.

• *Give instructions for tasks one at a time.* Children with ADD often cannot handle multiple commands and are confused by the use of complex language. Therefore use simple and direct language, providing instructions for a single task at a time until your child shows that she is capable of processing more than one instruction. In addition, preface your instructions with your child's name, as in "Marie, put your plate in the sink, please."

• *When giving oral instructions to a child with ADD, maintain constant eye contact with her.* And if you're not sure she's listening, ask her to repeat your instructions aloud.

• *Give instructions in statement form.* Many parents ask, "Are you ready to go to bed?" when they really mean, "It's time to go to bed." When you ask a question, the child may assume that you are willing to accept whatever answer you receive. While there are times when you certainly want to give your child choices, be sure not to mistakenly provide options when you do not mean to do so.

• *Encourage children to write daily "to do" lists for themselves.* Checking off items they have completed will give them a strong sense of accomplishment. Using a marker board can be helpful for maintaining current lists of things to do and upgrading lists easily.

• *When a child appears unmotivated to complete tasks, use a contingency approach:* "If you want to do such and such (have a friend spend the night, for example), you must do such and such first."

• *Remember: Children with ADD need regular routines.* Establish firm bedtimes, wake-up times, and study hours—and stick to them!

• *When angry, try to avoid yelling and punishing your child.* Instead, use Time Out (see p. 91) to help alleviate your—and her—frustration.

SETTING YOUR CHILD UP FOR SUCCESS AT SCHOOL: GENERAL APPROACHES

Many parents mistakenly believe that what happens to their children with ADD in school is beyond their control. On the contrary, you can play a major role in setting your child up for success in this arena as well.

Again, your role as advocate comes into play. Talking to and educating your child's school administrators and teachers about the special needs of your youngster with ADD is crucial, as is your willingness to help them find ways to help your child shine. Granted, this can be exhausting at times, but the fact is that an ADD child's success at school very often hinges on whether or not he has a parent willing to go to bat for him.

There are also steps you can take at home to set your child up for success at school. Here are some general guidelines to keep in mind:

• *Provide a quiet place free of distractions (no television or radio, and away from windows) where your child can do his homework.* Some children respond better working in the same place everyday. Others need a change of scenery to stay motivated and focused. In any case, always try a study setting for several days before concluding that it doesn't work for your child.

• *Use a study/office setting for homework, and work side by side whenever possible.* Your goal should be to get your child in the habit of working in a work setting. Kitchen tables, sofas, and the floor may be comfortable locations for the child, but they are also generally high-traffic settings and do not send the message "This is serious work that needs to be completed to the best of your abilities."

• *Check your child's backpack routinely and help him get organized.* Have a regular place for keeping books, notes, homework, etc.

• *Use a daily homework assignment sheet that the teacher initials daily.* Avoid putting all responsibility for getting it signed on the child, however, as he is using this approach because of difficulty remembering responsibilities. It's a good idea to have on hand the telephone number of at least one other child in your youngster's class—or, with permission, the teacher's home number—to call for clarification of assignments. Often it gets extremely busy in the classroom, and the teacher may not be able to check your child's assignment book on a particular day. Therefore it's best to be prepared with an alternative plan.

• *Review your child's homework assignments nightly to make sure she has completed all of them.* It's also a good idea to get your child accustomed to having assignments reviewed on a regular basis. The purpose of this is not to make sure that all of the answers are correct. Rather, you want to check that the assignment has been completed and that your child has made an effort to do it neatly. This provides parents with an opportunity to praise their child for good effort and to make recommendations for improvements the next day.

• *Limit homework to a reasonable amount of time.* By reasonable, we mean no more than two to two and one-half times the amount of time that primary-grade children are expected to spend on homework and no more than 50 percent more than the amount of time middle and high school students are expected to spend on homework. For example, if a third-grader's homework is expected to take about twenty minutes, a child should not have to spend more than forty to fifty minutes on that assignment. Similarly, if a tenth-grader has about an hour's worth of homework and studying, he should not need more than one and one-half hours to complete that work. You may need to consult with your child's teachers to find out how long they estimate students should spend on each assignment.

To help your child complete his homework more quickly within this reasonable amount of time, using a timer and allowing periodic breaks can be beneficial. Set the timer initially for five to ten minutes and encourage your child to work hard on the material until the bell rings. The timer should be sitting on the child's desk so that he has a visual reminder of the need to move along. When the bell rings, return to check over your child's work and progress. If he has done well, he can take a break for a few minutes. The clock is then set for thirty seconds to one minute longer than it was during the previous session, and the same procedure is repeated.

• *Number your child's assignments and worksheets or give them to him one at a time, so he doesn't feel overwhelmed.* Many children spend as much time shuffling papers around as they will trying to complete their assignments. Numbering a child's assignments or giving them to him one at a time helps him to become better organized and teaches him to organize himself.

• *If your child has trouble in one particular subject, hire a private tutor or "study buddy" to help him out.* Schools will often have a list of teachers and other adults who are interested in tutoring. Local high school and college students might also be interested in helping your child. In addition, there are numerous commercial tutoring firms that do a good job of motivating children and pinpointing their strengths and weaknesses. Many of these businesses have special training and experience working with children who have various types of learning problems. Whomever you hire, the more recommendations you can get in advance through other parents and friends, or by attending PTA or Ch.A.D.D. meetings (see the Appendix), the greater the likelihood that your child and the tutor will work well together and that the tutoring will be beneficial. Using a tutor also takes some of the pressure off of you and should diminish stress levels in the home.

• *Make yourself available to work with your child's teacher when your youngster needs extra help.* When you are unhappy with the quality of work coming home, when the teacher sends home many notes about your child's poor performance in school, or when you have other concerns about your youngster's work or behavior, it's wise to act quickly. Sitting around for weeks waiting for your child's report card or waiting for the teacher to suggest a conference may compound the problem, and the child's self-esteem suffers. Request a meeting with your child's teacher to talk about how all of the parties involved can help your youngster be more successful.

• *Run interference, if need be, with your child's teachers and friends when trouble erupts.* One of parents' most important roles is helping their child succeed. In this regard, the parent must be a "case manager" of sorts, monitoring the child's performance in school, in sports, in the community, and at home. When a problem occurs, ultimately it is the parent's responsibility to make things happen that will help get the child back on track.

• *Request that school administrators place your child in classes with the lowest student-teacher ratios and the most understanding teachers.* Clearly there are some teachers who work better than others with children who have ADD. They may be warmer, more structured, more sensitive. While school administrators may have a policy of not granting requests for specific teachers, if you provide adequate documentation demonstrating how your child has done over the years with different types of teachers—and if you are persistent in making your desires known—most school administrators will acquiesce to a reasonable request.

• *Ask that your child be given preferential seating away from windows and doors or other areas that can be distracting.* Just as with finding an appropriate place for getting homework done at home, it may take a trial and error approach to find the correct place to seat a child with ADD in the classroom. Procedures for preferential seating are described in more detail in Chapter 6.

• *Give your child's teacher ideas for special and creative incentives she can use to motivate your child in the classroom*—like reading to a kindergarten class, being a "big brother" or "big sister" to a younger child who needs tutoring, getting extra time on the computer, acting as class monitor, or visiting the library, if he completes his work on time.

PARENTS AS DISCIPLINARIANS

Parents of children with ADD, particularly mothers, often report feeling "torn"—totally dejected and ineffective in controlling their child on one hand, and extremely guilty about the anger they feel toward the child on the other. Many often question whether or not they really love their child, considering this constant frustration and conflict.

The problem is that children with ADD are *consistently inconsistent*. At times they can be extremely compliant and will follow your directions to the letter. At other times, however, they have a knack for pushing all the right buttons to get under your skin. The solution? Increased structure and clearer expectations will help you to become a more effective and satisfied parent.

Now that you have a good grasp of some general strategies you can use to motivate your child with ADD, let's delve into some more specific ways you can help your child become better—not only at following directions, but at meeting your, and others' expectations.

This section is the most important of the book, so read and reread it until you feel confident that you understand every strategy suggested.

BEHAVIOR MANAGEMENT STRATEGIES

In an effort to make sure their children with ADD follow directions, stay on task, behave in public, and keep up with their school work, many parents admit—often with a great sense of guilt—that they yell a lot or spank their children. Our behavior management approach includes neither of these measures. Rather, it places more responsibility on the child than on you to control his or her own behavior. In fact, it is structured to make parents more or less bystanders in the disciplinary process.

This behavior management approach encompasses several fundamental principles:

• *Make it clear to your child that the focus is on her behavior.* You can do this by constantly reinforcing the fact that you love *her*—what you don't like is her behavior.

• *Give your child choices* between demonstrating the correct behavior or dealing with the consequences if she chooses not to cooperate. That way, youngsters learn to make responsible decisions.

• *Deal objectively and promptly with inappropriate behaviors.* For example, if your child is touching something she shouldn't be touching, playing at the table with her food, throwing things around the house, or fighting with another child, you must intervene promptly rather than letting the behavior persist or escalate until you are frustrated and angry.

• *Ignore behaviors that are not dangerous and are not interfering with what your child should be doing.* If your child is slumped down in her chair while doing her homework, for instance, ignore her posture so long as she continues to work. In other words, if you pounce on every little behavior, you will generate more conflict than you resolve.

• *Make special efforts to let your child know when she is behaving or performing well.* Some parents of children with ADD complain that it's difficult to find anything that their child *does* do right, but what this often means is that the parents have stopped looking. Whether it's helping out around the house, politely answering the telephone, or greeting a neighbor, there are many opportunities to give credit where credit is due.

• *Caregivers must be consistent.* Once parents of children with ADD find behavior strategies that work at home, these should also be used by a child's other caregivers. Otherwise the child will be confused, and the goal of her being responsible for her own behavior will not be met.

However, when grandparents are intent on being permissive or when a noncustodial parent is unwilling to follow the plan, there are likely to be more setbacks. In such circumstances, continued structure at home will help the child to learn that the rules are always the same there, even though they may change elsewhere. The hope is that eventually the child will generalize what he gets at home and at school to other settings.

• *Help your child learn to monitor her own behavior.* By using such phrases as "boss yourself" or "check yourself out," you cue your child that better self-control is needed at that time. When used consistently, this approach helps the child become more aware of her behaviors and begin to assert greater control over herself. With academic tasks, help train your child to "check in with herself" at frequent intervals to evaluate if she has understood what she has just read, if she is making progress on her worksheet, if she is copying the sentences correctly, etc. For example, a child may learn to stop after each sentence she reads to be sure she understands it before moving on. This helps prevent her from getting to the bottom of the page and realizing she doesn't remember what she has read—a common problem for children with ADD.

• *Challenge your child to motivate herself.* Teach her to come up with ways to work faster or more efficiently. For example, if she got three questions correct on one reading comprehension passage, challenge her to answer four questions correctly the next time. Set a timer to see how long it takes her to complete one long division problem, then challenge her to do the next one in a little less time. If she needs a certain criterion for performance—such as completing a task within a certain period of time or a certain level of correct responses—help her to develop these. Have her think of and write down what she wants to do when she finishes her work. Be careful, though, to use this approach to generate greater success rather than greater failure. By setting up a model that spurs motivation, the child can then start setting up her own challenges and incentives to work more quickly and more efficiently.

THE CONTINGENCY APPROACH

Children of all ages have favorite activities—things they look forward to doing on a daily basis: watching a favorite television program, riding their bicycle, playing a computer game, calling a friend or grandparent, borrowing the car. The contingency approach utilizes a simple formula: Before the child can do what she *wants* to do, she must do what she *needs* to do—or what you want her to do. Here are some examples of how this approach can be used with children of different ages.

"Jonathan, if you want to watch your video, you have to eat six more bites of vegetables and finish your hamburger."

"Susie, you can go outside and ride your bike as soon as your room is cleaned up."

"Arthur, if you sit quietly in the cart while we're at the grocery store, we'll stop and get some ice cream on the way home."

"Sherry, if you want to go skating with your friends tonight, you have to get your term paper finished first."

"Alex, if you want to use the car to go to the mall, you

need to apologize to your sister for fighting with her
and show that you can treat her nicely."

This simple but powerful approach can be used with
children as young as twelve to eighteen months of age.
You must follow but a few necessary steps. First, you
must be able to identify the things that your child likes to
do most. Often youngsters will help you do this by making suggestions about things they like to do. However,
you must also be aware of activities they are looking forward to in the near future so that you can use these as incentives as well.

Second, the activities your child wants to take part in
must be timed appropriately. In other words, you can't
talk about an outing to the park on Saturday as an incentive if it's only Tuesday. In fact, as a rule of thumb, try not
to use an activity as an incentive if it is scheduled for
more than an hour or two away. In addition, the incentive
should not be elaborate or extraordinary. Those things
your child looks forward to on a regular basis are the
most desirable incentives to use.

Third, avoid using as a consequence an activity
you're looking forward to as much as—or more than—
your child. Say you've been counting on having dinner at
a new restaurant, and your child knows how much you're
looking forward to it. Saying to him "We won't be going
out to eat tonight if you don't clean up your room" won't
work. On the contrary, it places the child in the position
of being able to sabotage or control what *you* want to do
rather than you controlling what *he* wants to do.

Fourth, and most important, be consistent in following through on what you say. Do *not* change rules after you have made them. If you want your child to finish his homework before he goes outside, your job is to make sure that the homework is done before he walks out the door. There is no need for further negotiation or debate. The criterion is clear: The homework is either complete or incomplete.

Fifth, you must be willing to tolerate the child not doing what you want him to do while assuring that he does not get the positive consequence. With children who are extremely resistant to following directions, use the contingency approach at every opportunity. Consistency in using this approach—even for simple directions—helps the child learn that he must listen to what you say. Therefore, you can use even simple contingencies, such as the following:

"Malcolm, please put this glass on the table for me before I put the video in for you."

"Carlie, please put the pillow back on the couch, and then I will get you a drink."

As your child's efforts at following instructions improve, you can reserve the contingency approach for those tasks that create the greatest stress.

When children lose rewards, they may respond, "I didn't want to do that anyway." This is typical and is aimed at getting you to give in. Don't. Be strong, and know that the privilege or activity you've taken away probably *is* important to the child. And even if it means that homework doesn't get done for a few days or a room doesn't get cleaned up for several days, your youngster will eventually give in and show you that the reward was an important one after all. From your perspective, it's a matter of being willing to lose a few battles in order to win the war.

Again, when disciplining your child with ADD, it's important to remember that the message you send should be that you love *him* but don't like his *behavior*. Granted, many of us feel compelled to explain to our children all of the intricacies of why we do things a certain way. But this strategy appears to do little good and, in fact, may even harm children with ADD. Very often they will try to take advantage of your willingness to discuss disciplinary measures in an effort to manipulate the situation. It's their way of delaying meeting their responsibilities. It's also a way for them to control the situation.

You should recognize, however, that this type of behavior often results from the child's perceived inability to perform a task easily. That is, he recognizes that he has great difficulty sustaining his attention—say, on homework—for a long period of time, and it becomes very difficult and unpleasant for him. Likewise, he may recognize that he doesn't have the persistence to get his room cleaned up and is destined for failure if he is asked to do so. Consequently, his tendency is to battle against this kind of structure. Nevertheless, providing consistency on your part, as well as realistic and reasonable expectations along with support and reassurance, should soon result in greater success for him.

TIME OUT

On some occasions, a child's behavior becomes so disruptive, or you begin to feel so frustrated or angry, that the best approach is to remove him from the situation. The object of Time Out is to deprive the child of attention or positive reinforcement. Sitting your child in the corner, however, rarely works, since he needs only make noise, rock back and forth, or stand up to get your attention. Moreover this strategy is likely to encourage the continuation of his unacceptable behavior. Thus the best location for Time Out at home is in your child's room. As with the contingency approach, several principles should be followed:

Prior to sending your child to his room, follow this three-step approach. First, tell him clearly the kind of behavior you expect him to display or to cease displaying. Some examples:

"Brian, sit on the sofa quietly."

"Erin, stop fighting with Cynthia."

"Mark, go sit down at the table now and get started on your homework."

If the child does not comply, again state the behavior you want (or don't want) and indicate the consequences. Examples:

"Tonya, leave the knobs on the stereo alone, or you will go sit in your room."

"Eric, set the table now, or you won't be able to watch 'America's Funniest Videos' later tonight."

"Sally, clean up the mess you made on the kitchen table, or you can't go outside and play with your friends."

While it's nice to phrase *all* statements in positive terms, a "stop doing" statement is typically the first thing that comes to mind when a child is obviously not listening. These approaches should help reduce the number of negative statements you make.

Finally, if the child persists, send him to his room with the instruction "Stay in your room until you are ready to _____." Essentially, this approach makes the child responsible for deciding when he is ready to comply; at that point he can come out of his room.

Avoid telling your child to go to his room and think about what he did. Focus instead on the behavior that you'd like to see rather than what you saw. That way, when the child is in his room, instead of moping about what he's already done, he too can focus on the kind of behavior it will take for him to be able to leave the room. He can also then monitor whether he is ready to exhibit the kind of behavior you've requested or not.

If your child comes out of his room and continues to display the same disruptive behavior, send him back to the room again with the reminder that he can come out when he is ready to behave the way you want him to behave. This is the last chance you give him to change his behavior before resorting to other, more intensive disciplinary measures.

Again, make it clear to the child that you love *him* but that his *behavior* needs to change. Your message must be that you want to be with him but that first he must behave well. And he will have to stay in his room until he is ready to behave correctly.

What about children who refuse to stay in their room? In instances like these, the child recognizes that he can still control the situation by coming and going and getting attention from you for that. The following strategy may appear quite extreme. Nevertheless, it meets the criterion for a very sound behavior management program: it is not punitive, it results in an improvement of the child's behavior, and the child has control over administration of the consequences. Here is how the approach works.

Reverse the door knobs on your child's door so that the locking mechanism is on the outside. Then, after the child comes out of his room for the second time and continues to display the same disruptive behavior, you can send him back to his room and lock the door. Repeat your instructions: "You may come out as soon as you are ready to _____."

Once the child is back in his room for the third time and realizes that the door is locked, he may scream and bang or kick the door. Try to ignore his temper tantrum. You may also need to childproof the room as much as possible before using this procedure by removing any objects that might be breakable or harmful. But, again, do not allow the child out of his room until he is ready to behave the way you want him to.

Thirty seconds after locking the door initially, you can go back and ask if he's ready to come out and do what it was you requested. If he is not ready, walk away and come back in another minute and a half. Repeat this process about every five minutes thereafter. When he is ready to come out of his room, deal only with the behavior you requested of him previously. If he doesn't comply, send him back to the room and wait a little longer before checking to see if he is ready to come back out.

When you first begin using this approach, your child may spend a good part of the first few days in his room. However, once he realizes that he is not in the position of controlling the situation—and that you will be consistent—his behavior should improve.

Remember, harsh as this seems, this is not an inhumane approach. It may be difficult for you to continue the process, but your consistency is the key to the success of this method. Keep in mind throughout the ordeal that your *child* makes the choice of when he is ready to come out of the room, and that his choice is based on a desire to behave in an appropriate way.

Time Out can also be used effectively in public. At restaurants, at malls, and in supermarkets, children who are easily overstimulated generally demonstrate some of their worst behavior. The use of contingencies in these situations may be effective and should be tried first. However, you should avoid packing everyone in the car and heading back home unless dealing with the difficult behaviors by using various approaches has been ineffective, and you're frustrated and overwhelmed. Leaving the scene only reinforces the child's feelings of being able to control the situation and call the shots.

You can better deal with inappropriate behavior in public by taking the child into a bathroom or hallway and indicating that you will stay there until the child is ready to behave. The unstimulating environment of a restaurant bathroom might be all the encouragement a child needs to straighten up once he realizes that you are serious about your willingness to stay there as long as necessary. Realistically, this won't work if you're the only adult there with several children. And if that's the case, you just might need to avoid these situations, if possible, and concentrate on establishing control at home first.

Time Out is an effective strategy for a number of reasons. First, because it separates you and your child, it allows you to cool off and not get angry and frustrated. It also removes your child from a reinforcing environment. Second, Time Out places your *child* in charge of deciding when *he* is ready to improve his behavior. Third, and best of all, Time Out provides an opportunity to de-escalate situations that can easily get out of hand.

To make it work, however, you must intervene when a child first begins to behave inappropriately. If you wait until the behavior gets out of hand, it will be much more difficult to bring the situation under control.

Both the contingency approach and Time Out should be used consistently. They help the child structure his own behavior and provide some relief for parents who feel as if they are constantly on their children's backs. These approaches can also be tied successfully to other strategies—such as charts and daily allowances—we recommend using in specific situations. And since they can be equally effective on children without ADD, these strategies can be used to instill acceptable behavior in all of your children. That way, the child with ADD doesn't feel as if he is being singled out.

CHORE CHARTS

For children with ADD who are ages five and up, various types of charts can be a valuable asset in molding and reinforcing positive behavior. And when charts are tied to valued consequences, many children actually enjoy and often benefit from having the visual reminder. Here's how it works:

You and your child decide on no more than three behaviors or tasks that the child must accomplish before receiving certain privileges. These may include such goals as cleaning up her room, playing nicely with her sister, completing her homework, reading for thirty minutes, sitting quietly at the table and completing her meal, taking out the trash with just one reminder, being ready when the school bus arrives, etc. These consequences may relate to how many of the three goals the child accomplishes. For example, if she accomplishes all three goals, she earns all of the privileges. If she completes two out of three tasks, she may earn all but her most valued privilege (watching television, for example). If she does not accomplish any of the goals within a given day, she forfeits all privileges and, in addition, may have to go to bed thirty minutes early.

Whenever possible—or at least initially—consequences should be administered the same day. Later, weekly consequences can also be used, based on how many checks or stars the child has earned by week's end.

Suppose your son is given an opportunity to earn three checks in a day, or a total of fifteen during the five-day school week. If he is looking forward to seeing a movie with friends on Friday evening or going to a skating party on Saturday, he may have to earn at least twelve checks during the week to enjoy that privilege. Once a child has developed a pattern of responsibility and can accomplish these tasks without fuss and constant reminders, you can discontinue the chart or substitute new goals for old ones.

Be sure, however, to change the menu of consequences as your child's interests change. While it's not unusual for a youngster to say, "I didn't want to watch television anyway!" it's important that you remain persistent and tolerate some failures for a few days while working toward the larger goals of improved behavior and performance. For instance, if for a few days the child still decides that he can live without television, add some other privilege to the consequences that he can earn along with television time. That way, it shouldn't take long before the chart is doing the work for you, and your child becomes more responsible and easier to manage. Charts also provide you with additional opportunities to reinforce the pride you are taking in your child's good behavior. (See the Appendix for an example of a Daily Chore Chart.)

ALLOWANCES

Giving your child (ages five and up) money on a regular basis can teach her to be responsible with money. Allowances, however, should not be given without strings attached. Children should have specific responsibilities they must accomplish to earn the allowance.

Many parents of children with ADD have been successful using a daily allowance that is tied to responsibilities listed on a chart or to general performance. For youngsters who value their allowance and who need it to buy things they want, this strategy works well to reinforce positive behaviors.

CRISIS POINTS

Every family with an ADD child experiences crisis points—usually daily and often several times daily. By crisis points, we mean times the child with ADD is least able to get organized and to meet his responsibilities and when parents are most likely to become angry and frustrated: getting ready for school or day care, completing homework assignments, mealtime, bedtime, family shopping excursions or outings. These are common crisis points, and they are the most challenging times of day for both youngsters with ADD and their parents. Learn how to deal with them (by using the strategies we've discussed thus far), and you will feel more successful as a parent. Moreover, your child will gain greater feelings of control over his behavior and he, too, will feel more successful.

TAKE CARE OF YOURSELF!

Be honest with yourself and your family. If you're having trouble accepting the fact that your child has a disability, or have accepted it and feel angry or guilty about it, counseling can help. You might also consider joining a support group for parents of children with ADD; see the Appendix for more information. Many offer expert speakers as well as an opportunity to let off steam among other parents who share your predicament.

Above all, always try to understand your child's perspective on her problem. Just as her disability often leaves you feeling frustrated, humiliated, and guilty, she feels likewise. And as often as you feel helpless, hopeless, and out of control, so does she. But you can't let the downside of ADD tear the two of you apart. Rather you must work together to overcome the obstacles ADD tosses your way.

The strategies we have discussed can make a big difference at home and in the community. But they may not work all the time, particularly with children who are extremely disorganized, distractible, or active. While moving toward improving behaviors in your child, however, these strategies offer opportunities for you to alleviate some of your frustration, anger, and guilt. They are not a cure—there aren't any. But you will be amazed and pleased at how much life will improve for everyone with the added structure and consistency.

5

• • • • • • • • • • • • • • • • • • •

Medications and Other Treatments

Although eligible for public kindergarten, Brian was held back in preschool by his parents for an additional year. His teacher at the time suggested that Brian was immature and would benefit from an extra year in preschool. This year in kindergarten, his teacher has had frequent conferences with Brian's parents to indicate her concerns about delays in his development. She says that Brian's paper and pencil skills are less precise than other children's in the class, including those who are younger than he is. Neither is he learning letter names and sounds as quickly as she expects. In addition, she says Brian has trouble sitting still during story time and has more difficulty than other children staying in his learning center. When standing in line he can't seem to keep his hands off the other children. As a result, many of his classmates have learned to keep their distance from Brian so they don't get into trouble.

Brian's parents report that at home he is always underfoot. He has trouble playing by himself and shows an interest in books and other learning materials only when someone is sitting with him. At mealtimes, he is up and down at the table and is a very picky eater. When the family goes out to a restaurant or on a shopping trip, Brian is often very difficult to manage. "He can't seem to stay in one place and often wanders off without concern for his own safety," his mother reports. His parents add that Brian is often a very sweet and sensitive child, but that they spend much of their time feeling frustrated about his inability to follow directions that seem reasonable for a child his age. They claim they have yelled, spanked, taken away privileges, and sat Brian in the corner—all with little in the way of results.

Many professionals recommend that children with ADD receive some type of behavior therapy as part of a comprehensive treatment. This behavior therapy may take the form of parental training, self-control therapy, cognitive behavior therapy, social skills training, or some variation of these. Unfortunately behavior therapy alone generally is ineffective in controlling the symptoms of ADD with a child whose disorder is moderate or severe. The outcome for behavior therapy may be enhanced when it focuses on specific solutions to specific problems, such as learning how to organize materials or making daily schedules. But these programs often fall short in their ability to help the child generalize training from a clinical setting to a natural setting.

Because behavioral therapy strategies often don't transfer well from clinical settings to real life, behavioral interventions alone are often insufficient in helping children with ADD achieve success in their educational, social, and personal endeavors. In such cases—and after careful implementation and evaluation of numerous behavioral interventions—your physician may prescribe medication designed to modify the neurochemical errors in your child's brain. More than 80 percent of children with ADD who take medications show some degree of improvement.

The decision to place a child on medication for what appears to be a nonmedical problem is a difficult one for many parents. However, your child's current happiness and future success may well depend on your making a correct and timely decision. On one hand, you might hope that your child will outgrow the problem quickly— or that you will learn to tolerate his difficult behaviors. On the other hand, the child's inability to control his behaviors and to meet the reasonable expectations of school and home may well lead to feelings of despair and to a resignation to being a "bad" or "dumb" child.

The longer-term outcome for a child who has adopted this low self-image can be dismal. While parents may choose to assume the role of martyrs by putting up with the youngster's difficult behaviors, it does the child little good in the short term or the long term. Therefore, when behavioral approaches have failed to resolve the problems, it is usually in the best interest of the child to try medication and to commit to using it for a long enough period to determine whether or not it is effective. The logistics of the medication trial should be determined by the child's physician.

Here are some points to remember when starting your ADD child on medication:

• *Let him know why he is taking medication.* Children from the first grade on are aware that they are experiencing difficulty concentrating, controlling their behavior, being organized, getting along with other children, etc. They are often consoled to know that medication may resolve these problems.

Occasionally your physician may suggest that neither your child nor his teacher be told why the child is taking the medication. The reason for this "secrecy" is to help prevent what is called "treatment effect." Treatment effect occurs when a person knows that he is being treated for a certain condition and that the treatment is expected to cause certain changes. Sometimes the person expecting a change will alter his behavior voluntarily or subconsciously and cause some changes to occur, regardless of the actual effects that the treatment has or doesn't have. To avoid this treatment effect, physicians may ask that the participants in a medication trial be kept "blind" to the expected changes that the medication should have. Once this trial period is over, however, your child and his teacher should certainly be made aware of the reason for the medication.

• *Medication for ADD is generally prescribed ac-*

*cording to a child's weight. Nevertheless children of the
same size or age may require significantly different doses
to achieve the same benefits.* Moreover, as time goes on
and as children grow, it is quite common for them to outgrow a dose and for a regression in behaviors to occur. If
and when this happens, an adjustment in the dose may be
necessary.

• *Medications are typically started at a low dose and
increased gradually until an effective dose is achieved
with the fewest side effects.* With some medications, the
correct dose may be achieved in a matter of days; with
others, it may take several weeks or even months.

• *Although side effects usually are not serious, parents and teachers should monitor their children closely
and report to their physicians serious episodes of
headaches, stomachaches, lethargy (tiredness), tachycar-
dia (rapid heart beat), persistent difficulty getting to sleep,
persistent loss of appetite, tics, and mood swings.*

• *With the exception of a few medications that come
in chewable tablet form, pills should* not *be chewed or
ground up.* This may compromise the potency and consistent effectiveness of the medication. Your physician can
provide guidance on how to get a younger child to swal-
low a pill.

• *Some children respond differently to the generic
forms of ADD medication.* Thus it's usually a good idea
to start your child on the brand name. Once you've had
an opportunity to gauge the success of the medication, as
well as to establish a correct dosage, your physician may
consider switching to the generic form of the medication.

• *Avoid attributing normal developmental behaviors*

and behavior patterns to the medication. Once a child starts medication, parents often become alarmed by every behavioral episode that breaks the normal routine. Parents should realize that most children get into occasional fights, sometimes have sleepless nights, may not want what is served at mealtime or are not hungry, fail to bring home a book, or even blow a test. Only when a *pattern* of old behaviors appears is it time to consider what might be causing them and talk to your physician or psychologist to figure out how to get the child back on track.

MEDICATION FOR NONSCHOOL ACTIVITIES

Should your child take medication on weekends, holidays, after school, and during the summer? While physicians offer differing opinions, ultimately the deciding factor should be how well your child functions in his environment without the medication, balanced against the significance of side effects. For example, if your child exhibits poor self-control at restaurants, family outings, or at church or synagogue, continuing his medication might be advisable. Similarly, if your child spends his time during soccer and baseball games watching birds fly overhead or digging holes in the ground with his foot, it might be advisable to try him on medication during these times.

Your decision must be balanced against the undesirable side effects that the medication may have. If the use of medication late in the day interferes with your child's ability to fall asleep at night or causes such a dramatic decrease in appetite that there is a significant weight loss, it might be best to withhold the medication—or at least talk about other options with your physician or psychologist.

Medication is often critical during homework time. If the child's school dose wears off by then, a few brief assignments may take several hours to complete. This is also a time of day when everyone in the home is tired and has shorter tempers. Together with behavioral interventions described elsewhere in this book, homework time is an appropriate time for a trial with medication to see what benefits are realized. If homework time is typically spent arguing with your child, medication at this hour can enhance family harmony as well as provide your child with the extra time needed for recreational activities that he might otherwise spend anguishing over getting his homework done.

When trying to decide whether or not to try medication during homework time, keep these two criteria in mind: when behavioral approaches are ineffective, and when your child is unable to complete his homework in a reasonable amount of time. As we indicated earlier, by "reasonable" we mean no more than two to two and one-half times the amount of time that primary-grade children are expected to spend on homework and no more than 50 percent more than the amount of time middle and high school students are expected to spend on homework. If your child consistently requires at least that long or longer to complete his work—and requires your constant attention to help him finish it—it is appropriate to consider the use of medication.

TYPES OF ADD MEDICATION

The two main categories of medication used to treat ADD are stimulants and antidepressants.

Stimulant Medication

Stimulant medication appears to be the most effective therapeutic approach for treatment of ADD, particularly when combined with behavior management strategies. Why does stimulant medication work on a child who may already appear overstimulated? While it may seem counterproductive, stimulant medication appears to work by blocking the reabsorption of neurotransmitters from the synapse. This allows the more efficient transmission of nerve impulses in the brain and greater self-control by the child.

In fact, some 60 to 80 percent of school-age youngsters with ADD respond favorably to stimulant medications. Benefits include decreased impulsiveness and hyperactivity, and improvement in the child's attention span. Studies have also shown that ADD children taking stimulant medication are less aggressive, more compliant, and enjoy improved motor skills.

Ritalin is the most common stimulant medication used for children with ADD. It has a long history of use and a high success rate, and it results in relatively fewer side effects than other drugs used to treat the disorder. The generic name for Ritalin is methylphenidate hydrochloride, and a typical starting dose is 5 milligrams once or twice a day. Pills are available in 5-milligram, 10-milligram, and 20-milligram doses. Ritalin takes effect within about thirty to forty-five minutes and usually lasts for three and a half to four hours. These pills may be cut in half to adjust doses.

Ritalin also is available in a 20-milligram sustained-release (SR) form. This pill cannot be cut or divided and often requires a little longer to take effect, but it should last approximately seven hours. The absorption of the SR dose often is less consistent than with the fast-acting dose. Benefits from using an SR dose may include fewer behavioral peaks and valleys during the day and elimination of a noontime dose—of particular value to middle and high school students who are sensitive to the stigma of taking pills at school. A single-dose approach is also of value when the child does not get the pill at school consistently. Often fast-acting Ritalin is added to an SR dose to provide the best coverage through the day.

When a child does not respond well to Ritalin—or experiences too many side effects from the drug—doctors often prescribe Cylert (pemoline). Cylert is taken once a day, in the morning. The starting dose is usually 18.75 milligrams or 37.5 milligrams. Unlike Ritalin, a therapeutic blood level is achieved slowly. Several days to several weeks may pass before the noticeable effects of the drug appear.

Children who do not respond to Ritalin or Cylert may respond to Dexedrine (dextroamphetamine). This drug is used less often now than in the past, primarily because of its reputation as a "street drug" when used in higher doses and because it is less available. Since it came in elixir form, it was once preferred for young children, but it is no longer available in this form. Dexedrine comes in fast-acting tablets and in time-released, long-acting capsules (spansules). The starting dose for Dexedrine is generally 2.5 milligrams, about half the starting dose for Ritalin.

Unfortunately, many newspapers, magazines, and television talk shows have attempted to sensationalize stimulant therapy. Naturally this alarmist approach has left many parents unwilling to try a treatment program that has dramatically improved the lives of children with ADD symptoms for more than fifty years. (See: "Setting the Record Straight" below for a comparison of myths versus facts regarding stimulant therapy for children with ADD.)

SETTING THE
RECORD STRAIGHT

What are some of the misconceptions surrounding stimulant medications?

Myth: *Stimulants cause dangerous side effects ranging from permanent brain damage and severe depression to growth retardation and Tourette's syndrome.*

Fact: There is no scientific evidence to indicate that stimulant medications cause brain damage or severe depression. Studies do, however, indicate a very slight effect of stimulants in slowing children's growth. But, as with all medications, individual children respond in different ways to the same type and dose of medication.

The most common side effects of stimulants are decreased appetite and insomnia. Other side effects of stimulants include headaches and stomach aches. In rare cases, a child may experience extreme agitation, rapid heart rate, and liver problems. Side effects often cease after a few days or with a decrease in dose or change in medication.

Tourette's syndrome may be unmasked as a side effect of Ritalin. But since Tourette's syndrome is a hereditary condition that involves vocal and motor tics, there is usually a family history of the disease. Your child's doctor should be notified if the disease exists in your family, so that he can closely monitor the child's use of Ritalin or prescribe an alternative medication.

Myth: *Stimulants aggravate hyperactivity in ADD children.*

Fact: Occasionally, a parent may notice what experts call a rebound effect in their child when the medication is wearing off. The youngster appears extremely restless and may be more difficult than ever to control. This usually occurs in the late afternoon and can last for thirty to forty-five minutes. It doesn't mean that the child is reverting to a premedication state. Nevertheless many physicians who once limited their ADD patients' dosages of stimulants to school hours are now prescribing an extra dose later in the day to help youngsters maintain control through the late afternoon and early evening.

Myth: *Stimulants cause children to exhibit "zombie-like" behavior.*

Fact: Stimulants, by nature, do not have a tranquilizing effect. However, too large a dosage may cause a child to be lethargic. Consequently, if a child appears glassy-eyed or complains of feeling overly tired and down in the dumps, his dosage likely needs to be adjusted. Be sure to contact your physician before changing a dosage.

Myth: *Stimulants are addicting.*

Fact: There is no evidence to suggest that this is true for children with ADD when they are carefully monitored. In most instances, youngsters remain on the same dosage for years; in fact, many get by with a lower dosage as they grow older. Furthermore, when children with ADD forget to take their medication—or their parents opt not to administer it on weekends or vacations—children show no symptoms of dependence.

Myth: *Taking stimulants puts children at greater risk of becoming drug or alcohol abusers later in life.*

Fact: Because children with ADD are more impulsive, they may be more prone to experiment with drugs and alcohol. But it's their disorder that puts them at risk, not their medication. In fact, evidence suggests that when stimulants have a positive effect on a child's behavior, he feels more in control of his life and receives more positive feedback from others. As a result, his self-esteem soars, which makes substance abuse far less likely.

Monitoring a Child on Stimulants. For a child to receive maximum benefits from stimulant therapy, physicians usually encourage parents to take charge and closely monitor their child's progress. Here are some guidelines for the use of medication as your child begins his treatment plan:

• If your child is just starting stimulant therapy, give the first dose on a weekend. That way you can monitor any immediate side effects and look for positive changes.

• Always follow your physician's directions.

• Let your child try going without medication on weekends and vacations. Keep his medicine handy, however, in case he needs it. (Be sure your physician has agreed to its use at these times.)

• Tell your child's teachers that he is taking medication so that they, too, can be on the lookout for side effects and report benefits.

• Some children do fine on one dose per day; others need additional doses to stay focused throughout the afternoon and evening. If required, a second dose should probably be given at lunchtime. Set up a schedule with your child's doctor.

Antidepressants

When stimulants are found to be ineffective, physicians will often try treating ADD children with antidepressants. The most commonly used medication in this category is Tofranil (imipramine), which is also used to control bed-wetting. A starting dose of 25 milligrams per day is typical. Because overdoses of antidepressants are far more serious than those of stimulant medications, careful supervision and monitoring of a child's response to these medications is extremely important.

Tofranil works much like a stimulant medication in that it blocks the reabsorption of neutrotransmitters at the nerve synapse. But the effects of Tofranil are not immediate. Generally it takes two to three weeks before optimal therapeutic effects will be evident.

Other types of antidepressants that may be used for ADD are Prozac (fluoxetine), Norpramin (desipramine), Elavil (amitriptyline), and Pamelor (nortriptyline).

Other Medications

Doctors have recently begun experimenting with an antihypertensive drug called clonidine (brand name Catapres). While this drug has not been used extensively with children, there is some evidence that it is effective with youngsters who have frequent temper tantrums, or in situations where other medications produce undesirable side effects. It may also be beneficial with children who show signs of anxiety and depression along with ADD. Clonidine appears to work particularly well for youngsters who have ADD together with Tourette's syndrome or other tic disorders.

Clonidine is started on a gradual basis and may be increased up to about .2 milligrams per day. In addition, when the medication is stopped, it must be tapered off gradually. One of the benefits of using clonidine is that at maintenance doses it can be administered via a transdermal patch. The youngster wears each patch for seven days and receives a constant dose of medication during that period of time. One of the drawbacks to this approach, however, is that many children develop severe skin irritations from the adhesive that attaches the patch to the skin.

The most common side effects from clonidine are a decrease in blood pressure, sleepiness, dry mouth, and nausea. It may take several days to several weeks before beneficial effects are observed with this medication.

Other types of medicine that have been used in a more limited way with ADD are Corgard (nadolol), an antihypertensive drug; Buspar (buspirone), an antianxiety drug; and Tegretol (carbamazipine), an anticonvulsant medication.

MEDICATION FOR LIFE?

Youngsters who take medication to help control ADD continue this therapy for different lengths of time. Deciding if and when medication should be stopped is based on the child's ability to control his behavior on his own. In other words, as he matures and becomes more aware of his behavior, he may find himself more in control.

In general, by the time a child reaches kindergarten or first grade, he is aware of his behavior, but he is not yet equipped with the skills necessary to maintain control of himself. By fourth grade, children's self-awareness is far more heightened, and peer pressure becomes a factor as well. Consequently at this age youngsters may begin to show levels of self-control and self-discipline to compensate for ADD without medication. Of course, the only way to determine whether or not a child can get along without medication is to compare his performance in similar situations on and off medication. For this reason, physicians often plan intermittent drug holidays to observe how the child handles himself in various settings without medication.

Since medication is prescribed according to body weight, dosages must often be adjusted as children grow older and larger. If, however, a child continues to do well on his current dose, a change in dosage probably is not necessary.

By helping to keep them focused and in control, medications can have a tremendous impact on children with ADD. But their treatment cannot stop there. In fact, sometimes the rapid improvement in a child's attention span has unpleasant outcomes. He may become more aware of his academic problems and more attuned to the difficulties he has experienced with other children. This can lead to increased sadness and even signs of depression. Or he may begin to show a keen interest in new activities his parents consider insignificant.

Neither of these situations should alarm parents. They simply demonstrate the fact that, to reach their fullest potential, children with ADD need time as well as help and support from both their parents and others outside the home, such as school counselors, educational administrators, and teachers.

REMEMBERING MEDICATION AT SCHOOL

The issue of medication compliance becomes a significant one when a child is supposed to take several doses during the day, with at least one of them at school. Some schools prefer placing responsibility on the child to remember to go to the office to get his medicine. However, it is because of the child's poor organization skills and sense of forgetfulness, in part, that he is taking the medicine! Therefore placing the responsibility on the child is setting him up for failure.

Making teachers responsible for a child taking medication has its drawbacks as well. They often have so much going on in the classroom at once that they may often forget to remind the child that it is time for his medication. Teachers also may have many children in the class who take different medicines on different schedules. Keeping track of each child becomes a difficult process.

Several approaches can be used to help assure that your child receives his medication on a daily basis:

• Tie taking medication to a specific daily activity. For example, have your child stop at the office for his medicine on the way to lunch, on the way back from the computer lab, etc.

• Ask the school nurse (if there is one) to help remind the child.

• Consider buying your child a digital watch with an alarm. Set the alarm for the time when the child is to report to the office for his medicine. Be sure that his teacher is aware that the watch will beep at that time and that the purpose is to make the child responsible for following his own schedule.

CONTROVERSIAL TREATMENTS

Several new kinds of treatments are currently being used for children with ADD that are considered controversial.

Many of these approaches have been scrutinized by researchers and scientists and found to be lacking in a number of ways. Most appear to work, based on anecdotal information from parents, but their success has not been documented in published research reports.

Documentation published in research journals satisfies a number of necessary requirements that should be met prior to acceptance of a treatment. First, it provides a specific description of strategies used in treatments. This information helps practitioners gain a better understanding of the conditions under which a certain approach may or may not work. Second, it describes the individuals on whom the strategy was used. The success of the strategy with a certain segment of the population does not necessarily mean it will be useful with other individuals. Third, published research should compare the results of using an approach to changes in the individual when the approach is not used. This practice of using "controls" allows practitioners and other scientists to look at the actual changes that occur when the approach is used and compare them with variations and changes that occur naturally over time.

Fourth, to conclude that an approach works, a large and well-defined sample must be used and appropriate statistical analysis applied. Fifth, research papers are traditionally submitted to other professionals for their review and critique prior to a paper being published in a journal. This peer-review process provides a standard whereby research reports that do not meet the necessary professional criteria generally will not be published and consequently will avoid misleading readers. Finally, documentation should also contain evidence that other individuals who use the same approach have achieved the same results. If one researcher reports that a certain technique works but no other researcher is able to duplicate the results, it provides false hopes for parents and skepticism among professionals.

Many different treatments fall into this category of controversial treatments:

Neurofeedback

Advocates of this approach indicate that there are changes in brain electrical activity, as measured by electroencephalogram, when neurofeedback is applied. Specifically, proponents believe that attention, focus, and concentration can be improved, together with task completion and organizational skills, impulsiveness, and mild hyperactivity. The few published reports available on this treatment, however, do not clearly define how the treatment is used. Nor do they use large enough sample sizes or control groups. Replication of results has also been insufficient to support the widespread use of this approach.

Diet

Diet therapy to treat ADD has received greater attention from the media than have treatments supported by published research reports. Unfortunately, there is little evidence—aside from anecdotal reports—that an additive-free diet, an allergen-free diet, or any other idea that calls for removing certain food items (such as sugar) makes any consistent difference in the child's behavior. This does not necessarily mean that a dietary approach should not be tried. There probably is a small percentage of children who, in fact, would benefit from diet modification. For example, there has been some evidence to suggest that young, very active males stand to benefit. However, diet management should fall under the supervision of a physician who will monitor the child's general health, weigh the child regularly, and conduct periodic blood tests. In any case, the wise parent is one who naturally limits the quantity of "empty foods" that a child eats—such as ketchup, artificial drinks, chocolate, etc.

Orthomolecular Approach

Advocates of this approach believe that certain genetic abnormalities produce alterations in the child's need for, or metabolism of, certain vitamins and minerals. Unfortunately, there is little consistent support for the strategy of providing ADD children with vitamin and mineral supplements. Both the American Psychiatric Association and the American Academy of Pediatrics have stated that supplements make no difference in the behavior of a child with ADD.

Yeast Control

Another proposal is based on the idea that at least some of the behaviors associated with ADD are the result of excessive growth of yeast in the body. Consequently proponents of this approach recommend the use of medications—such as Nystatin—to control yeast growth. However, no research to date supports this claim.

Sensorimotor Integration Therapy

Two recent approaches relate to the vestibular system, including organs in the inner ear and cerebellum, which advocates of this approach believe causes poor integration of brain functions and consequent organizational problems, attention problems, and other difficulties. One approach recommends the use of anti-motion sickness medication or antihistamines combined with stimulant medication. The other is based on sensory integration theory. In brief, this theory proposes that nerve pathways in the cerebrum, the thought-processing and information storage part of the brain, can be altered by stimulating the vestibular mechanism in the ear. While this particular approach may work with some children who have certain kinds of learning disabilities or neuromuscular problems, there is no research evidence that either of these approaches benefits children with ADD.

Cognitive Interventions

A number of cognitive strategies have been proposed that claim to decrease a child's impulsiveness and improve attention and self-control. The most successful of these is self-monitoring, in which children are trained to track and monitor their own behavior. Other approaches—such as self-instruction and anger-control training—appear to be ineffective. In fact, most cognitive strategies tend to transfer poorly from clinical to real-life settings.

PARENT BEWARE

Many individuals have gotten wealthy preying on the frustrations of desperate parents. There are always people hopeful that the next "solution" that comes along will be the answer to their problems. Please be cautious and conservative when someone claims they have a cure for ADD. The truth is that there are no cures for the disorder, and that is not likely to change for quite some time.

In this chapter, we have tried to present an objective description of therapeutic approaches that do work, as well as those that do not. The important thing to remember before trying any approach is to be sure to speak with professionals familiar with it and with a cross-section of parents who have used or considered the approach. Attending a Ch.A.D.D. meeting (see Appendix for information on this organization) or another parents' self-help group will also help you gain more information in this area.

6

● ● ● ● ● ● ● ● ● ● ● ● ● ● ● ● ● ● ● ●

The Role
of Teachers

Jenny, a fifth-grader, has missed recess for nearly two consecutive weeks. Her teacher knows how much Jenny likes to play outside and is trying to encourage her to earn back this privilege. The problem? Jenny's name has been on the board every day for nearly a month—for not turning in her homework assignments on time, for turning them in incomplete, for talking too much in class, and for picking on the other children in her class at lunchtime.

Jenny's teacher is confused. She sees Jenny win class

spelling bees and can't understand why she consistently scores in the low 70's on written spelling tests. She watches Jenny complete math problems perfectly on the board and so is confounded when the majority of Jenny's answers on written math tests are incomplete or incorrect. She is always telling Jenny, "I know you can do better," yet Jenny insists that she is trying as hard as she can.

Like the parents of children with ADD, teachers also experience confusion and frustration about these children's attitudes and abilities. And with good reason. In some instances, the child with ADD appears bright, capable, and motivated; in others, she appears lazy and uncommitted to accomplishing her goals and objectives. Because of this inconsistency, some teachers instinctively blame the child for her poor and sloppy work, repeatedly insisting, "I know you can do better than that." Or they point the finger at the child's parents and encourage them to be more firm and strict with their offspring.

Parents, in turn, will tell their youngster's teachers how hard they have worked to support their child with ADD. They will explain how they have attempted to be more restrictive by depriving their children of privileges, by putting them in Time Out and, in some cases, by spanking them. None of these measures, they will likely add, has worked effectively. They will also recount the number of hours they have spent helping their child finish a homework assignment that should have taken just minutes to complete.

The problem is that unless teachers fully understand what ADD is and how it affects its young victims, they cannot appreciate the fact that the child's problem is with what she *shows* rather than what she *knows*. For example, once teachers realize that the child can work well on an individual basis and orally, they will learn to credit the child when she demonstrates her skills in these ways. Teachers with a solid knowledge of ADD and its effects will also soon discover that results of traditional testing typically understate what the ADD child has learned. Most importantly, once a teacher finds the flexibility and strategies to help the child with ADD succeed and feel successful both academically and socially, the child and her parents will feel encouraged as well.

PARENTS AS EDUCATORS

ADD children are constantly on the receiving end of messages from adults that say, "You are a problem and a disappointment." Consequently, when teachers write messages on an ADD child's paper such as "Sloppy—do over" when it was the child's best efforts, or "This is easy work—you need to study more" when the child and her parents spent hours the night before preparing for the test, it reinforces the child's feelings of incompetence. As a result of these persistent messages over several years of schooling, the child eventually becomes resigned to the fact that she is incapable of meeting her own—or anyone else's—expectations.

Many of the children eventually give up their unsuccessful attempts to please others and to accomplish personal goals. Some may become oppositional and then exhibit severe conduct problems. Others may begin to show signs of apathy and depression. Moreover some children, whose impulsive behaviors allow them to do things that are contrary to their value systems (like stealing), may begin lying as a defense mechanism to preserve some degree of self-esteem.

That's why it is critical for parents to make sure that their children's teachers not only understand ADD but do all they can to help those children succeed in their classrooms. Most teachers are familiar with ADD, but many do not know the cause or its effects or how to implement strategies that can improve these children's behaviors and performance. That's where you can help.

First, make sure that your child's teacher has a thorough understanding of ADD. A good first step is sharing "What Is Attention Deficit Disorder: A Guide for Teachers" (see page 129) with each of your youngster's caregivers and instructors at the beginning of the school year. Next establish a good working relationship with your child's caregivers and teachers. Let them know that you are able and willing to serve as a resource for them by providing suggestions for strategies they can try in the classroom to help both your child and others with ADD succeed. Finally study the "Strategies for Success in the Classroom" section in this chapter carefully so that you can serve as a knowledgeable advocate for your child—and as a resource for his teachers.

Keep in mind that your child's response to the different approaches a teacher uses to remediate problems in the classroom will vary based both on the severity of your child's problem and his age. Therefore, you may find that one or two of the strategies we discuss will help to resolve many of the classroom problems your child is experiencing. Or you may discover that using all of the strategies still does not bring the child up to a level of performance high enough that he experiences academic success or increased feelings of self-worth. Nevertheless it is a teacher's obligation to try classroom modifications prior to suggesting a consultation with a physician for consideration of medication. And while you don't want to be pushy when suggesting some of these ideas to your child's teachers, you may have to be politely firm and insistent.

WHAT IS ATTENTION DEFICIT DISORDER? A GUIDE FOR TEACHERS

Attention Deficit Disorders (ADD) affect between 3 and 10 percent of all school-age children and is four to eight times more common in boys than it is in girls.

There are two broad types of Attention Deficit Disorders. One is characterized by hyperactivity and impulsiveness. These youngsters are generally easy to identify in the classroom. They are out of their seats frequently, move around the classroom more than other children, and have trouble staying in one place. Children who have ADD characterized by chronic inattentiveness, on the other hand, may be more difficult to pinpoint. The most common characteristics to watch for include daydreaming, not completing seat work, difficulty getting started on seat work, poor organization skills, and frequently losing and forgetting things.

Children with ADD have difficulty following instructions; forget to write down homework assignments, even after being reminded repeatedly; don't hand in assignments, even when they have been completed; and don't appear to be motivated, as other children are, by incentive programs. Dig a bit deeper, however, and you may be surprised to find that the child is capable of doing more than what a superficial evaluation indicates. For example, if you call on a child with ADD when she appears to be daydreaming, she often has the right answer. If you sit down with her to redo a unit test on which she received a 42, she may surprise you by getting a 96. And if you call her up to the chalkboard to do a problem that she missed on a worksheet, she is likely to answer it correctly. These discrepancies in performance make it imperative for teachers to be particularly patient and understanding with children who exhibit symptoms of ADD.

Very often ADD occurs in conjunction with other problems. For example, many children show impairments in written language (penmanship), spoken language (including word retrieval and fluency), memory, and reading. Some children meet the diagnostic criteria for depression or oppositional disorders. It is unclear at this time how the problems are related, but the good news is that the symptoms of these secondary problems sometimes improve when ADD is successfully treated.

Help Is Available

In recent years, school systems have made numerous resources available to you, in both print and other media, to help you work with these children in your classroom. In addition, the Student Support Team structure helps to provide better communication within the school system by assisting with monitoring the child's progress, by preparing him or her for formal psychoeducational testing, if needed, and by offering a way to get the child's parents involved in more structured ways for dealing with the comprehensive needs of the child.

What to Look For

What can you do if you suspect that a child has ADD? Suggest that the parents contact their family pediatrician to discuss medical options while educational interventions are being evaluated. And when should you suspect ADD? There are a number of checklists available that assist in testing your suspicions. Keep in mind, though, that *ADD is a medical diagnosis that can be made only by a physician*. Most physicians, however, will welcome and solicit your input in helping to differentiate between ADD and other problems that may manifest similar types of symptoms.

An ADD Checklist

The following questions can assist you in validating your suspicions that a student has ADD. All evaluations are made relative to other children of the same age.

1. Does the child appear to daydream or is he easily distracted?

2. Does the child have difficulty sustaining attention on tasks, particularly seat work?

3. Does the child have difficulty getting started on seat work?

4. Does the child often fail to complete work but give responses at the beginning of the task that are often correct?

5. Does the child consistently respond better orally in class discussions than on paper and pencil evaluations of the same material?

6. Does the child fidget a lot, playing with papers, pencils, zippers, etc.? Does the child sit in unusual postures (leg folded under, for example)?

7. Does the child perform better one on one and in smaller groups than when working independently or in a whole-class activity?

8. Is the child impulsive, doing and saying

things before he thinks? (This may include calling out in class, pushing another child, providing off-the-topic answers to questions, etc.)

9. Does the child have difficulty getting homework assignments written down, taking home the correct books for homework and studying, carrying notes back and forth between home and school, etc.?

10. Has the child not responded to being held in from recess, assertive discipline strategies, and incentives for improved performance?

11. Does the child do poorly on classwork and not hand in homework, even though his parents indicate that they spend considerable amounts of time working with the child each evening at home?

There are numerous variations in the performance patterns of children with ADD. For example, many children do extremely well on tests even though their day-to-day performance is extremely poor. However, if the answer to most of these questions is yes, it is advisable to assume that the child has Attention Deficit Disorder and to implement appropriate strategies until a definitive medical diagnosis is made.

STRATEGIES FOR SUCCESS
IN THE CLASSROOM

When individualized strategies are suggested for use in working with a child with ADD, one concern that teachers often raise is that other children will feel left out or slighted. Fortunately this is an empty argument. Children are often far more insightful than adults and are quick to realize individual differences in their peers. In fact, they often become one another's strongest allies. Therefore, when help is provided to a child who has difficulty staying in her seat, finishing her work, or participating in classroom activities without undue disruption to the class, her classmates will understand. For most children, the satisfaction of completing a task, getting a good grade, and "fitting in" is sufficient reward to keep them happy and productive in the classroom. When additional intervention is needed for one or two other children in the classroom, they will raise no objection.

In applying intervention strategies, suggest that your child's teacher start with one strategy and try it for several days before evaluating its success. After that, another strategy can either replace the first or be added in stepwise fashion until your child's performance improves to an acceptable level compared to other children in the class, or until all strategies have been tried and been found to be unsuccessful. Obviously you'll have to rely on the teacher's judgment to determine the best combination of strategies, how long to continue with each one, and how to make them work for your child in her classroom.

But be sure to touch base with her periodically to see how things are progressing.

For children in upper elementary grades and beyond, where several teachers are involved, make sure that all of your child's teachers use similar strategies for the same types of problems—unless, of course, your child's problem is manifested in different ways with different teachers. In that case, each teacher should use strategies that best meet the individual needs of that classroom, teacher, and your child. In middle school and high school, it is often wise to identify one contact person—a homeroom teacher, school counselor, or assistant principal—with whom to maintain contact.

Preferential Seating

Placement in the classroom of a child with ADD should be chosen carefully. Some children will perform better when seated near the teacher's or paraprofessional's desk. Others will do best sitting closest to the chalkboard or in the front of the room. Still others will perform better when they are seated in the middle of the classroom or near other children who can serve as work models for them. In any case, the criteria for successful placement should be: improvement in copying materials from a chalkboard, beginning work more quickly, staying on task to complete seat work, paying attention during teacher-led activities, and decreased distractibility and inappropriate interactions with other students.

Increased Vigilance During Unstructured Times

Social problems (pushing, throwing objects, taking objects from others, etc.) among children who are impulsive tend to increase during the less structured times of the school day—transitions from one activity to another, during lunch, between classes, while at recess, and in physical education class. Therefore during these times greater supervision by adults can often head off potential problems and prevent a child with ADD from making a foolish mistake.

Study Buddy

With twenty-five or more students in a class, teachers often have a difficult time giving a distracted child the amount of attention needed to keep her working productively. Furthermore, when a child's name is repeatedly called out and accompanied by negative messages, it can be equally frustrating to both the child and the teacher. Often, making statements such as "I like the way _____ is working" (using the name of another child who is demonstrating good work habits) will help the child with ADD get back on task. But even this may be a futile effort in the long term. Therefore seating the child next to an ambitious but subtle student is often beneficial. Give responsibility to that child to assist the youngster with ADD to stay on task, have the correct materials out, and keep the right place during class activities. The ideal study buddy is one who can do this in a matter-of-fact way without calling undue attention to the student.

Organizing Work

There are a number of ways a teacher can assist the poorly organized child in getting started on seat work or in completing assignments. First, worksheets or assignments can be numbered, so that rather than shuffling papers or books for twenty minutes in an effort to decide which to do first, the child completes them in numerical order.

Second, the child can be given just one worksheet or assignment to complete at a time. When completed, she delivers it to the teacher or paraprofessional, who gives approval to move on to the next task. Third, the child can keep a list on her desk of assignments to complete, and she can check them off as she completes them. Although a similar list may be on the chalkboard, the nearness of an individualized list may be necessary to help the child with ADD become better organized.

Finally, a timer may be placed on the child's desk and set for a reasonable amount of time for her to finish a given task. Often the visual reminder, along with a specific allotment of time provided, will help the youngster get started on a task more quickly and complete it more efficiently. The amount of time to provide for a task should be left to the discretion of the teacher; however, it should be long enough to assure the child an opportunity for success but short enough to provide a mild challenge.

As days pass and the child achieves success, the amount of time should be shortened for similar types of tasks.

Adjusted Workload

Many children with ADD are easily overwhelmed both by papers with a great deal of writing on them and by complex tasks. While the intent of reducing a child's workload is not to have lower academic expectations of her, it may be necessary—at least initially—to reduce the amount of work the child must do to demonstrate that she knows the concepts that are being taught. On math worksheets that have twenty-five problems to complete, for example, the last ten problems may be no more difficult than the first fifteen. Therefore, if the child completes only ten to fifteen of the problems rather than all twenty-five, she is still demonstrating a knowledge of the math concepts. Similarly, if the class must write or correct ten sentences to indicate a mastery of appropriate punctuation, the child with ADD can demonstrate the skill by doing half of those sentences. The purpose of this approach is to allow the youngster to experience success, while acknowledging that she has mastered the skill or concept but is unable to sustain attention long enough to complete the longer assignment. Over time, of course, the intent is to increase the workload as the child shows increasing ability to do longer assignments. In addition, the child should learn to self-monitor her quality of work and task completion during this process.

Grading Work

It is frustrating for a child to try his best and continue to earn poor grades because he is unable to complete the work. When your child with ADD shows a consistent pattern of incomplete papers and assignments, encourage the teacher to either cut down the length of the work or to grade only what your child has completed. This provides your youngster with an opportunity to get graded for his knowledge and skill of the material rather than for his inability to sustain attention on his work. An alternative to this approach is to have the teacher hand the paper back to your child at a different time and allow him to complete the rest of the assignment without penalizing him. It is important to recognize that for preschool children as well as high school children, it is disheartening to consistently receive sad faces or red F's marked on papers when the child is making his very best effort and really knows the material but is unable to control inattention and distractibility.

Unfinished Classwork

If your child is not completing work in the classroom and thirty minutes of homework is already taking two hours or more to complete at home, a teacher sending home additional work to complete merely transfers the crisis from the classroom to the home setting. This also places an unfair burden on you and unrealistic demands on the child, who should have some time each day for recreation. Parents often look to teachers as the experts in dealing with these kinds of problems. But when the teacher shifts that responsibility back to the parents, it breeds greater frustration and anger in the parents, who may feel "dumped on." In such instances, you'll need to work closely with your child's teacher to negotiate ways in which your youngster completes enough of his work to be graded fairly, but not so much that he is forced to become a young—and frustrated—workaholic.

Incentive Systems

Teachers of young children often use incentives such as stickers, end-of-the-week parties, and other treats to motivate students to do their best. For children with ADD, the rewards for doing work may need to be provided on a shorter-term basis, and the menu of incentives may need to be varied. For older children, the types of incentives may need to be modified (e.g., special computer time, the chance to act as bus monitor or raise and lower the school flag, etc.), but the use of incentives can still be effective for increasing productivity and feelings of self-worth.

There are numerous approaches to incentive systems. All variations focus on the child's positive behaviors and efforts rather than on breeches of the rules alone. Offering desirable incentives with reasonable expectations for performance lets children feel that they can be successful and even benefit from extraordinary efforts.

Immediate Tangible Rewards. A child may receive a tangible reward, such as a sticker for completing a specific task or assignment within a given amount of time or for demonstrating a particular behavior such as staying seated for a specific amount of time. The criteria for success for the child should be challenging yet reachable, and more easily accomplished earlier in the program. For example, the child may get a sticker each time he stays in his seat for a fifteen-minute period or for each worksheet he completes during seat-work time.

Token Economy System. A token economy system offers immediate feedback with delayed gratification. Using this system, the child receives a token or marker to indicate that he has met some criterion. However, the child must accumulate a certain number of markers prior to receiving a reward. The markers may be lines on an index card on the child's desk, Popsicle sticks, buttons, etc. The child then has a menu of rewards for which he can cash in these markers when he has accumulated enough of them. The menu should have items with different point values and should consist of tangible items and activities that the child particularly enjoys. These might include stickers, pencils, time at the computer, a trip to the library, an opportunity to read to kindergarten children or to be a peer tutor, a trip to the principal's office for a treat, a free homework pass, etc. The token economy system for positive behaviors is a valuable one to try, particularly when the name-on-the-board approach and missing recess do not work. Menu items should be varied weekly and created in consultation with the child so that items that are most valued by the youngster are on the menu.

Classroom Segregation

At times, separating the child with ADD from the rest of the class may decrease distractions and provide the youngster with greater control over his work habits. It is best for teachers to deal with the issue in a straightforward way. In other words, they should talk with the child about his tendency to have trouble getting work finished when he is with the group and offer him the opportunity to sit at a table or study carrel positioned in a way so that there are the fewest visual and auditory distractions. When reading groups are going on, for example, the child should be placed as far away from the reading group as possible to complete seat work. Otherwise, the auditory distraction will hinder productivity. Similarly, a special table can be turned to face a corner or wall so that the number of visual distractions are limited. In general, the child should have the opportunity and freedom to go to that table when he feels it is necessary to complete his work. Some youngsters, however, may need to be encouraged to move to the table when it is apparent that they are not completing their work.

For many children, the use of a study carrel with barriers in the front and on the sides or a cut-out refrigerator box with the desk placed in it may be useful. To destigmatize its use, the teacher should give other children an opportunity to use it for specific projects and tasks. Allowing the child an option to work while standing or using a lectern or high table may improve productivity as well. After all, the purpose of segregation in the classroom is not to punish the child but to allow him opportunities to be more successful and to teach him how to modify his own environment to enhance productivity.

Homework Issues

When it comes to homework, numerous problems plague children with ADD. They often forget to write down homework assignments. They forget to bring home the books they need to complete their homework, and they often take three to four times as long as other children to finish the same homework assignment. Moreover, when they complete their homework, they often forget to pack it in their backpack or to hand it in the next day. Here are some strategies you and your child's teachers can try:

Homework Pad. Most children have a special place where they write down their homework assignments. In the early grades, teachers often provide a photocopied sheet that indicates the assignments for the day or for the week. For the child who consistently leaves school without his assignment written down, the teacher will probably need to see that the child has a sheet like this and that it goes into his backpack. Or the teacher needs to look at the written assignments entered on the child's homework pad and initial that it is complete and correct. Expecting that a child will remind his teacher to do this at the end of the day is setting the child up for failure. Think about it. The child is using this strategy because he forgets to write down the assignment. So it is just as likely that he will forget to ask the teacher to sign the pad. Therefore, at least initially, the teacher or paraprofessional should be encouraged to remember to ask the child for the pad.

Missing Materials. Children who rarely remember to bring home the right books for homework or for studying, or children whose desks consistently overflow with papers that should have gone home days or weeks earlier, should be instructed to empty the contents of their desks into their backpacks daily. While this may be a physical burden, it ensures that all books and papers the child needs to take home leave the school. As youngsters become more successful at demonstrating responsibility in the classroom, they can be weaned from this chore.

Location of Homework Assignments. If your child is doing his homework at night but the teacher claims that he is not handing in assignments consistently, call a strategy session with the teacher. Work together to devise a system whereby your child's homework papers will be placed in the exact same place in his backpack every night before school. That way, if the child doesn't hand in the homework on his own, the teacher or the child's study buddy can check in that specific location every morning to find it.

Limited Homework Time. As noted earlier, children with ADD can take hours to complete a brief homework assignment. Yet parents feel obligated to assure that the child does all his homework and feel guilty when he goes to school with unfinished assignments. Find out from your child's teacher how long homework should take. If you are consistently spending more than twice that length of time to help your child finish his homework, suggest that modifications be made. The most reasonable approach is that your child spend no more than two to two-and-a-half times as long on homework as other elementary school children and not more than 50 percent longer than older children. You might send a note to the teacher indicating how much time was spent on the homework and that it was not completed in that time frame. Your youngster can then be graded on what he completed or be given an opportunity to complete the homework in class.

Teachers can also help you find appropriate ways to structure your home environment so there are incentives for the child to get his homework done as quickly and correctly as possible. For example, maybe your child should not be allowed to go outside to play, watch television, play video games, or drive the car until his homework is done. However, when your child is unable to complete his homework in a timely manner—even with these incentives—modifications should be made in length of assignments.

Daily Report Card

A teacher's expectations that parents control their child's behavior or work habits in the classroom are unrealistic unless the parents are present in the classroom. Logically, a school's professionals should address events that occur during the school day. There may be times, however, when linking school and home performance is necessary. A good example is when school incentives do not appear to be working but the child has many activities to which she looks forward at home each day. On these rare occasions, using a Daily Report Card may prove useful. The Daily Report Card is a type of token economy system that offers home consequences of school performance. (Examples of Daily Report Cards for elementary, middle, and high school-aged children are presented in the Appendix.)

In general, here's how a daily report card works. The teacher rates the child at the end of each class or school day based on classwork performance, conduct, and whether or not the child handed in homework completed the previous night. Grades of A, B, C, D, and F, or S (Satisfactory) and U (Unsatisfactory), are given. If the child receives all satisfactory grades, she earns all privileges at home that day once her homework is completed. This may include going outside to play, watching television or playing video games, borrowing the car to run errands, etc. If the child gets one unsatisfactory grade for that day, she loses the most valued privilege at home for the remainder of that day. Finally, if the youngster receives more than one unsatisfactory grade or comment, she loses all privileges and must go to bed early that evening. The next day, the child starts over with a clean slate.

If the child fails to bring home the form, claims that the teacher did not fill it out, or offers any other excuse why she could not present it to her parents, it is treated as if there were unsatisfactory grades or comments on the form. This teaches the child responsibility and prevents the use of excuses to avoid consequences.

Student Support Team

School systems in every state are obligated by law to have a Student Support Team (SST) structure. Teachers who have been actively involved in the SST process know that the success of the team depends on the leadership of the group and on the openness of members to carefully analyze each child's problem and consider all possible alternatives. For the child with ADD who has no indication of a mental handicap or learning disability, interventions may include those described in this chapter or, in rare instances when a teacher cannot or will not implement reasonable strategies, a change of class.

The SST is also the pipeline for psychoeducational testing and special education services. Granted, children with ADD often do not qualify for traditional types of special education classes, but a case of ADD that does not respond to intervention and that seriously impairs the child's ability to learn may make the child eligible for other health-impaired special education services or services under Section 504 of the Rehabilitation Act. In any case, the SST process should focus on involving all parties productively in helping the child to be more successful in school-related activities.

MANAGING THE CHILD ON MEDICATION: A TEACHER'S ROLE

Teachers play a vital role in managing children who take medication for any reason. When a child is prescribed medication for ADD and it is not taken as prescribed or is omitted altogether, it is not the physical health of the child that suffers but her self-esteem, as well as the tone of the whole educational environment. The teacher's personal feelings about medication should be put aside when she is faced with a child who is not responding to behavioral interventions and who clearly is not meeting expectations.

As discussed in Chapter 5, numerous types of medication are used with children who have ADD. While many come in a time-release form and some can be administered by a transdermal patch that the child wears, some of these drugs must be administered several times a day.

Physicians will often begin children on medication by way of a blind study. That is, they may start the child on medication without the teacher knowing it, or they may intersperse the real medication with a placebo to determine the true effect of the medication. It is extremely important, therefore, that your child's teacher watch carefully for alterations in the child's behavior within a given day, as well as from one day to the next. The use of a log book or log sheets often serves as excellent documentation to verify the difficult behaviors the child exhibits, as well as to later reflect any benefits that the child shows from various types or doses of medications. The log should also include comments about the child's activity level, her ability to pay attention and work, and notes about interactions with her peers. The teacher should begin a log as soon as she notices unusual behaviors and prepares to begin an intervention strategy. An example of a teacher's log book appears on page 150.

Many children who are anxious about school complain about headaches, stomach aches, and other problems. Children with ADD often are among this group. Therefore, it may be difficult for teachers to differentiate the complaints of a child experiencing side effects from ADD medication from those who see school as a frustrating and unpleasant place. Side effects that are most common from medication used for ADD are headaches and stomach aches, loss of appetite, lethargy, and increased irritability. Communicating this information to your child's teachers and educating them on what to watch for will enable you to compare their input with that provided by your child's physician regarding side effects for the type of medication your child is using.

When children are supposed to take medication several times a day and forget to take a dose, both the child and those around her may suffer. Missing a noontime dose of Ritalin, for example, may cause increased distractibility and activity level during the afternoon hours, as well as generally poor performance. It is important that the child take medication at the prescribed times, even though it may interfere with her participation or be difficult for a teacher to remember to send her to the office to get her medicine.

SAMPLE: TEACHER'S LOG BOOK

2/6 (Wednesday)
Amy was ten minutes late to school. Seemed in good spirits but did not turn in all of her homework. Sat quietly and listened well when guest speaker spoke to class. Seemed alert and asked the speaker good questions. During lunch Amy was reprimanded twice—once for breaking in line and once for talking too loudly at the table. After lunch Amy appeared restless and could not seem to concentrate on her math test. Handed in her paper with only half of the test completed. At recess Amy and a classmate were put in Time Out for calling each other names. After recess Amy performed well in class spelling bee but couldn't settle down after that. She kept getting up to sharpen her pencil, get water, etc.

2/7 (Thursday)
Amy on time this morning but turned in only half of her homework. Seemed very tired. Said she didn't sleep well last night. Fell asleep at her desk during morning seat work. Barely touched her food at lunch. Said she wasn't hungry. After lunch

complained of headache. School nurse gave her some Tylenol. Amy seemed irritable the rest of the day. Asked to sit out during P.E. Didn't seem interested in any classroom activities today.

2/8 (Friday)
Absent.

2/11 (Monday)
Good day overall. Turned in her homework. Sat quietly and watched movie with rest of the class in the morning. Enjoyed music class. Helped me put up a new bulletin board before lunch and seemed pleased with her contributions to the effort. Ate well at lunch. Played well with peers at recess. After lunch was a bit restless during social studies. Finished nearly all of her math problems. Volunteered to play the lead in a class play we're planning. Became hard to manage as we were preparing to go home. Had to be told several times to pack her backpack and straighten her desk.

2/12 (Tuesday)
Another good day. Turned in all of her homework. Was proud to make the highest grade in the class on a spelling test. Behaved very well on our class field trip. Had minor problems at recess when classmates made fun of the way she played kickball. Worked hard for nearly an hour writing an essay for social studies. Did not finish her essay but asked if she could complete it at home overnight. Behaved extremely well in art class.

One way to help a teacher out in this regard is to suggest that your child take her medicine routinely in conjunction with a change in activities. Maybe she could stop by the office on the way to lunch every day or on the way back from the computer lab. You may offer to get your child a digital watch with an alarm; the watch can be set for the time when she should go to the office to get her medicine. Work with your child's teachers to devise strategies that draw as little attention as possible to your child when she must take her medicine, and find ways to place as much responsibility as possible on your child to monitor herself in taking it. Keep in mind, though (and remind the teacher), that the reason your child is taking the medicine is for the very problems that may prevent her from remembering when it's time to take it. Expecting your child to remember on her own consistently is setting her up for failure.

A FINAL WORD

Children with ADD cannot succeed in school without the understanding and flexibility of their teachers. Moreover, children's experiences in school affect both their life at home and their futures. Therefore, it is your role as a parent to do all you can to assure that teachers are educated about this disorder and are sensitive to the impact their approaches have on these special students.

ADD is not just the child's problem. It is not just the parents' problem. Nor is it just the school's problem. It is as pervasive and as potentially debilitating as the most severe mental or physical handicap. It takes away the child's desire to face a challenge, strips him of his self-esteem and self-respect, and may even cause him to question his reason for living.

Hopefully, as teachers become more informed about the disorder, they will be better able to help children with ADD experience success in spite of the disorder. They will be better able to help youngsters with ADD understand, accept, and compensate for their shortcomings. And they will be better able to offer you sensitivity and hope.

7

●●●●●●●●●●●●●●●●●●

Is ADD
Forever?

*T*hree years ago, Jake barely graduated from high
school. His parents had always promised him a
college education, but Jake had had enough of
school. "I was tired of studying so hard and then making
all C's and D's," he says. So Jake found a job in construc-
tion.

After a year on the job, Jake decided he didn't want
to spend the rest of his life building houses. He applied to
a small junior college and was accepted. "The classes
were small, and students got a lot of personal attention,"

Jake says, "so I thought if I worked hard, I could do well." But with so many social activities going on around him, Jake found he couldn't concentrate on his studies, and by the end of his first semester he was on probation.

The next semester, he passed one course but failed two others and was suspended. "I went back home to look for a job," he recalls. "My parents were disappointed in me, and I was disgusted with myself."

Over the next six months, Jake quit one job and was fired from two others. "I felt so restless," he says. "I couldn't concentrate on anything. Finally, my parents suggested that I seek professional help, and my mom made an appointment for me to see a psychologist."

Following testing and an analysis of Jake's school and family history, the psychologist diagnosed Jake as having ADD. "Neither my parents nor I had ever heard of ADD," he says. "But as soon as my doctor listed the symptoms, I knew I'd had it since about second grade."

Six months ago, at the age of twenty, Jake began taking Ritalin. "It's made a tremendous difference in my life," he says. "I can concentrate at work. I can relax at home. I feel better about myself than I have in years."

Jake recently began taking evening classes at a nearby community college. "Believe it or not, I'm studying psychology," he laughs. "I know it might take me forever to reach my goal of becoming a psychologist, but I feel sure I can make it. It's my dream to someday be able to help children who have ADD—so they don't have to go through the years of hell that I did."

Jake's story is not unusual. Countless adults had ADD as children but were never—and may still not be—

diagnosed. More often than not, their life stories sound a lot like Jake's: Many have trouble holding a job, have persistent mood swings, and display impulsive personality traits.

But what about those who are diagnosed with ADD as children? Do they outgrow their disorder? Until recently, most researchers and physicians believed that the symptoms of ADD became less pronounced once victims reached adulthood. However, what appears to happen instead is that the manifestations of the disorder change. Children with ADD tend to become less active, fidgety, and inattentive as they grow older. But studies of adults who were diagnosed with ADD as children indicate that between 30 and 70 percent continue to show symptoms that may have a substantial impact on their ability to function as adults.

Symptoms may include an inability to sustain attention to tasks, poor organizational skills, inability to finish projects and activities, and procrastination. Many adults with ADD have difficulty sitting through long meetings and waiting for traffic lights to change. They may also lose their tempers easily and get into fights with family members and fellow workers. Stressful conditions produce extreme levels of anxiety, anger, or confusion. Symptoms of depression may also appear in response to extreme levels of unresolved frustration.

Clearly the adult with ADD may face the same type of failure and unsuccessful experiences that children with ADD face. Frequent failures can perpetuate feelings of poor self-esteem, can lead to use of drugs and alcohol, and can cause marital and job stress. It is probable that adults with ADD are more likely to be unemployed, divorced, and substance abusers.

Ms. O'Neill, for example, was referred to the psychologist to help her ten-year-old friend, Jenny, a child with ADD who was struggling in school and at home. Jenny could not seem to get organized. If her mom did not sit with her in the afternoon, Jenny would plant herself in front of the television set or wander around the house. In school, Jenny's teachers reported that Jenny often appeared "lost in space." As Ms. O'Neill learned more and more about ADD from various professionals with whom she came in contact—and from publications and Ch.A.D.D. meetings she had been attending—she began reevaluating her own life.

As a young child Ms. O'Neill had been abused. She struggled through school, although everyone always considered her to be a bright child. She married shortly after her graduation from high school and had two children. Her husband was an alcoholic, and the marriage ended in divorce. Ms. O'Neill worked in a job where she was given many high-level responsibilities—ones far beyond the general expectation for the position she held. Her supervisors and peers recognized that Ms. O'Neill was a very capable and responsible individual. Nevertheless, she always harbored feelings of self-doubt, was restless, and felt mentally disorganized. Managing all of these feelings required enormous energy. But Ms. O'Neill was determined to meet others' expectations of her—even if it meant struggling—because she felt it was important to do so for the sake of her children and to keep her job.

Finally Ms. O'Neill made an appointment with a psychiatrist who had recently begun seeing adults with ADD. While Jenny continued to receive treatment for ADD, Ms. O'Neill was started on Ritalin. The effects were dramatic. She reported that close friends and associates noticed a difference in her without knowing that she had started taking medication. Ms. O'Neill reported a calmness and clarity of thinking that she had never experienced before. She was also able to better understand her daughter's problems and offer strategies for helping Jenny improve both in school and at home. Both Jenny and her mother appeared to be on the road to a brighter future.

Are there certain factors that contribute to more positive outcomes in adulthood for children diagnosed with ADD? Possibly. Children with ADD who have higher IQs and higher socioeconomic status tend to fare better as adults. The same is true for those who come from stable families and who are less aggressive. Studies indicate that children who were hyperactive are more prone to emotional problems as adults than are children who did not have ADD. Studies also reveal that hyperactive children tend to grow up with low self-esteem, work in lower-paying jobs, and have lower status, primarily because they are less educated.

Findings from studies on the effects of treatment on children with attention deficits are unclear. Some indicate that treatment of more than two years improved the outcome for these children. One study in particular examined the effects of stimulant medication used for two to five years in elementary school. The results indicated that the outcome for children with ADD in adolescence was

no different than for other children. However, as young
adults, the children who had stimulant therapy appeared
to have slightly higher self-esteem and social skills. When
adults were asked to look back and identify what most
helped them get through childhood, the majority cited an
individual within or outside the family who served as a
mentor or as a source of encouragement for them.

The results of recent research point out the need to
identify children with attention deficits as early as possible and to provide support and encouragement at all ages
to keep these youngsters on track. Stimulant therapy is
but one approach that improves a child's attention and
decreases behaviors that can interfere with success.
Equally important is teaching young children coping skills
and sound organizational skills that will contribute to improved feelings of confidence and high self-esteem. It is
important, too, to get the child involved in activities
where he can be successful, whether these are related to
academics, sports, the arts, or other areas.

Those diagnosed with ADD in childhood may have
to continue stimulant therapy through the adolescent
years and even into adulthood to be able to cope with
problems of disorganization, restlessness, poor concentration, and mood swings. But together with the adult's
higher level of maturity, these medications may provide
the key to helping an individual feel more competent and
be more successful at home, on the job, and in the community.

It is clear that for a high percentage of children with
attention deficits, life will always be more of a struggle
than it is for other individuals. What will sustain them

during these struggles and challenges are feelings of optimism that have foundations in their early years. It takes a team effort—parents and other family members, teachers, physicians and other health-care providers, and peers—to help build a happy and productive life for a child with ADD. Step back every once in a while and appreciate how worthy the effort is!

8

● ●

The Many Faces
of ADD:
A Collection of
Case Studies

T his chapter features a number of actual case studies of real children with ADD.* These case studies show the various ways in which the disorder can be manifested in different children. The notes and comments section that follows each case illustrates the variety of treatments that can be used to help youngsters with ADD—as well as their parents and teachers—cope with the disorder.

---

*Children's and other family members' names have been changed to protect their privacy in this chapter and throughout the book.

CHAD

Chad, five and a half years old, attends kindergarten at a public elementary school. Because of difficult and disruptive behavior at home, his parents had Chad screened at a mental health hospital to identify possible emotional problems. The screening process, during which a psychologist interviewed Chad and had his parents complete a checklist, revealed that Chad needed additional tests to pinpoint his specific problems.

Chad's parents describe him as a very active and loud child. They say he stays up late at night, has slept with them nightly for many years, and has a bed-wetting problem. Chad's father is an alcoholic, and there is a great deal of fighting between his parents at home. Chad is an only child who likes to watch cartoons and play outdoors. When he is indoors, his mother describes him as "always into something." Chad also has a mild articulation disorder in which he substitutes the *w* sound for the *r* sound, saying "woom," for example, instead of "room."

Chad had been getting into trouble consistently since the beginning of the school year. Notes from his teacher, describing both his disruptive behavior and the approaches she had used, were a daily occurrence. His teacher had tried Time Out, positive reinforcement, one-on-one discussion, restriction of privileges, and other reasonable approaches. Nevertheless Chad continued to have a difficult time sitting still for activities and completing tasks. At group table activities, Chad was constantly out of his seat, distracted away from the activity, speaking out of turn, misusing materials, and wandering away.

A behavior management strategy was applied at home to structure Chad's bedtime routine. The first step in the plan was designed to make his parents feel more in control of Chad's behavior, as well as to give them some extra time in the evening that was free of direct caregiving responsibilities. Chad was given the choice of sleeping in his own bed with the door open or with it closed. His parents reported that Chad slept in his bed all night by the second night of the program. They were also given suggestions regarding bed-wetting: cutting out fluids after 7:00 P.M. and having Chad empty his bladder before going to bed. While his bed-wetting decreased, it did not disappear completely.

Chad's parents adopted other behavior management approaches, including use of the contingency approach and Time Out. Both reported feeling more competent in being able to use these strategies successfully. However, Chad's behavior did not improve substantially in school or at home. Consequently, a trial on Ritalin was begun.

His parents began giving Chad the medication on a weekend and noticed a dramatic change in his attention and activity level. These positive changes continued into the school week, except that there appeared to be a regression in his behavior in the late morning, just prior to his second dose of the medication. After a trial of moving the second dose up an hour, it was determined that this would not provide sufficient coverage for the entire school day. Therefore, the morning dose was increased slightly and the noontime dose kept the same. This strategy provided excellent results and allowed Chad to do well academically, behaviorally, and socially in school.

Notes and Comments

When a child shows multiple problems relating to such things as bedtime, mealtimes, interaction with friends, and academics, a plan must be developed to address all of these concerns in an organized manner. While medication may be effective in addressing some aspects of the problem, it is not a substitute for sound and consistent behavior management strategies. Nor should it replace other traditional approaches for dealing with such things as bed-wetting. Both immediate and long-term success may well depend on more than just dealing with the problems that are most apparent and disruptive to the parents and teachers. Good solutions begin with a realistic evaluation that considers the comprehensive needs of the child within the family, the school, and the community.

RICHARD

Six and a half years old, Richard is in the first grade at a public school. Last year in kindergarten, Richard was having difficulty getting his work done and paying attention in class. Because he was overweight, some of the other children made fun of him, and Richard was unable to make friends. In addition, his teacher would constantly send home notes about Richard's poor behavior. She would also send Richard home with all of his incomplete and sloppy papers to complete and redo. Home became Richard's school away from school, and the majority of his afternoons, evenings, and weekends were spent trying to finish his papers. After two months of this, his mother decided to teach Richard at home. She figured that, at the very least, home-schooling might shelter him from the taunting of other students and his very negative teacher.

Soon, however, his mother discovered that Richard had a hard time working for more than fifteen or thirty seconds on a task without becoming distracted and wanting to get up and move around. Academically Richard did extremely well, but paper and pencil tasks and focusing on written and spoken material for long periods of time were difficult for him. His mother tried a number of strategies—brief breaks after short segments of teaching, interspersing passive and active tasks, and using a multi-sensory approach. Still Richard's problems persisted.

Richard was tried on Ritalin but showed a significant decrease in appetite and had difficulty falling asleep. Since he was overweight, the decrease in appetite did not pose a risk, but his difficulty getting to sleep was quite severe. After numerous adjustments in dose, Richard was tried on Cylert. This appeared to provide considerable improvement in his attention with fewer side effects. For the remainder of the kindergarten year, Richard was taught at home and made excellent progress. He returned to public school at the beginning of the first grade. But his problems were not over.

Despite the fact that his mother took great pains to describe Richard's characteristics from the outset of the first grade, his teacher frequently sent home notes and made Richard redo all of his papers when they were sloppy or when the spacing was not perfect. Soon Richard began tearing and shredding up his papers or rolling them up in a ball and stuffing them in his desk.

Richard never earned Friday treats, which were reserved for children who demonstrated good behavior and work skills throughout the week. Although he talked about wanting to earn treats and was disappointed when he didn't, he was never able to reach that goal. After a few weeks of trying his best to earn a treat, he confided to his parents that he didn't think he could ever do it.

His teacher's notes reported that Richard made noises in the classroom, would get up to sharpen his pencil numerous times during the day, and had the messiest desk in the class. Richard still managed to make good grades, despite the fact that he was forced to redo his work time and time again. His grades in conduct and handwriting, however, were unsatisfactory.

A Student Support Team meeting was requested. Richard's parents, his teacher, the assistant principal, and a peer teacher attended. His parents, who had two other children at home and were expecting their fourth child in a few weeks, took great pains to describe how they withstood many of Richard's less disruptive behaviors. "When we go to church, Richard squirms in his seat and makes a lot of noises, but we have learned to ignore those behaviors because that's just Richard," his mother reported. "If we got on him for every one of those behaviors, he wouldn't have a chance to breathe without us pointing out something he was doing wrong. We tried saying things like, 'Richard, sit still and be quiet.' But in less than a minute, he'd be doing the same thing. He just can't help it."

Richard's teacher listened with skepticism. "Well," she said, "we can't have that kind of behavior in the classroom. If I didn't put a stop to it quickly, all of the other children would start behaving that way." The assistant principal pointed out that since the teacher had not been able to put a stop to Richard's behavior quickly or any other way, perhaps other strategies could be identified to redirect Richard's inappropriate behaviors without sending continuously negative messages to him. It was suggested, for example, that Richard be given an opportunity to assist other children in math and reading once he had completed his own seat work. Considering that he was a bright child and at the top of his class academically, maybe he needed the social interaction and would feel good about having the opportunity to help other children. The group concluded that this might be a way to motivate Richard to complete his work quickly and to avoid other disruptive behaviors.

Richard's medication level was increased, and he was taught techniques to try to help him gain better self-control. These strategies appeared to have a positive effect. However, his teacher did little to change her approach in the classroom, and had Richard's performance not improved as a result of these other strategies, a trial period in another classroom would have been recommended.

Notes and Comments

There is little to gain by developing an adversarial relationship between parent and school. On the other hand, parents have a right to stand up for the best interests of their child when they feel that he is not benefiting from the educational environment. They should have some confidence that educators are interested in the welfare of their child, and this should be reflected in the efforts of the school to exhaust all strategies to help the child adjust and succeed in that setting. When things are not working, the parents should ask the question, "What can we all do?" And after having an opportunity to try out a different strategy, they should ask, "Did it work?"

Failure to follow through on suggested strategies may result in frustration at both ends. Parents may feel that the school is not doing its share to carry out what was proposed. School personnel may also be frustrated that the parents are not following through on commitments they have made. At times such as this, especially when the child is not experiencing improvement, it is often beneficial to seek the help of an outside person who can view the needs of the child in a more objective way. Finding such a person is the parents' responsibility. The person may be another parent, a psychologist, a counselor, or other individual familiar with ADD and school matters.

ALAN

Alan is fourteen years old. From infancy on, Alan's parents have described their son as a difficult child. Compared to his brother and sister, as an infant he was more fussy, slept fewer hours, and ate less. His parents remember Alan frequently waking up crying during the night and being extremely difficult to console.

During the toddler years, when Alan could not play outside he would mope around the house. He also had a difficult time staying clean and dry during the day until he was nearly four years old, and he continued to wet his bed almost nightly until he was eight.

As Alan grew older, he had a difficult time keeping friends. When he was in second grade, his parents, concerned about his poor growth and continuous reports from teachers about his inattention and inability to complete work, took their son to the nearest university medical center for an evaluation. After a thorough medical evaluation, plus a review of behavior checklists by his parents and a narrative report from his teacher, Alan was prescribed hormone therapy for a growth disorder, along with Ritalin. After a period of dose adjustments of Ritalin, the supervising physician changed his prescription to Cylert. The growth hormone therapy was discontinued after three years, but Alan continued to take Cylert with inconsistent results.

Now in the eighth grade, Alan has had a history of increasing problems over the years. His progress is now being followed by a pediatrician rather than the medical center. His parents say Alan has started fires, broken into a neighbor's house, stolen a bicycle, and done poorly in school. These behavioral episodes have been sporadic, but his poor academic performance has been consistent over the years.

Reports from current teachers indicate that Alan behaves well in school and has no apparent problems paying attention and completing his work. However, they say that Alan does not appear very motivated and often will not hand in his homework or take the time to answer questions completely.

A daily report card was initiated with rapid and positive results. With performance in class tied to recreational privileges at home, Alan's grades improved dramatically after just a few weeks. He also admitted to being pleased with the change and attributed it to the use of the daily report card.

Following this success, the parents and Alan cancelled or failed to appear for many of their scheduled appointments with their psychologist. Six weeks after his last contact with Alan and during the spring vacation, the psychologist received a call from Alan's mother. Her son and some of his friends had broken into a home in the neighborhood and stolen money and other goods. Alan's mother was frantic. She and her husband had been extremely proud of their son for the improvements he had recently shown in school. His mother was now distraught over what steps to take in dealing with the current problem.

Notes and Comments

Alan's case reflects a number of very critical points relative to children with ADD. First, ADD may coexist with numerous other problems and disorders. In addition, the persistent impulsiveness and frustration that is a part of ADD may contribute to other problems such as conduct disorders and delinquent-type behavior. Finally, parents often feel that when the attention problem and the most significant current problem appear to be under control (in this case, poor academic performance), contact with the professional is no longer needed.

Alan is small in stature, which was the reason growth hormone therapy was prescribed and which contributed to his feelings of inadequacy. Many children who are small for their age look to a peer group for acceptance. And, unfortunately, the maxim "Birds of a feather flock together" often pertains to children who have problems. Associating with other difficult children, together with a tendency toward impulsiveness, was a combustible combination that kept Alan in trouble.

It is not surprising that the episode of breaking into someone's house occurred during vacation time. Alan's academic performance improved when increased structure was added. During school days he had a very regimented routine that helped him to be more successful. However, during vacation the structure was gone. His parents let down their guard, and consequently Alan reverted to greater impulsivity. In addition, Alan did not take his medication, which is consistent with drug holidays recommended by many physicians for children who are on chronic medications.

Alan's pediatrician indicated to his parents that he would no longer write refills for medication unless Alan's progress was being monitored by a psychologist or counselor. The parents, shaken by their son's recent setback, agreed to their pediatrician's stipulation.

In spite of the financial burden of ongoing medical

care, Alan's parents felt reassured that they would now have somewhere to turn to avoid or to better deal with crises that arose. In fact, Alan had continued to make excellent progress, and his parents have had many opportunities to be proud of each of their three children.

JAMIE

Jamie is a three-year-old whose parents have experienced severe marital problems. Jamie's mother recently filed for divorce because of her husband's physical and emotional absence from the home and because of his unwillingness to spend much time with their son. Jamie's mother was troubled and frustrated by her son's behavior. She had recently taken him to a department store, and the manager asked her not to return because of Jamie's destructive and disruptive behavior. She revealed that no matter where they go, Jamie misbehaves. He runs away from her at the mall, wants to touch everything at the grocery store, is constantly interrupting her when she is on the phone or visiting with friends, and always touches things at home that he's been told are off limits.

Jamie's mother is very health-conscious and has been systematic about keeping her son away from artificial substances, chocolates, sweets, and other dietary items that might contribute to his high activity level and impulsiveness. This approach has not improved Jamie's behavior. She has also used Time Out and has awarded or taken away privileges contingent upon Jamie's behavior.

Because of the severity and consistency of Jamie's

poor behavior, a trial on stimulant medication was recommended. Jamie was started on a low dose of generic Ritalin (methylphenidate hydrochloride). After three days, his mother saw no change in her son's behavior. The morning dose was increased slightly, resulting in only a mild change in behavior. Before abandoning this strategy altogether, Jamie was started on brand-name Ritalin. The first day his mother reported that Jamie appeared wide-eyed and lethargic. However, on the second and subsequent days, she saw a dramatic improvement in his performance. She had several meetings set up with lawyers to discuss her pending divorce, and Jamie sat quietly at the lawyer's office reading and writing while she had her meetings. She had never experienced this pleasant occurrence with Jamie before. No side effects of the medication were noted.

Notes and Comments

Various behavioral interventions and diet management should be tried before using medication. Moreover, while use of medication with young children is less desirable than with older children, it must be considered when the behaviors are severe enough to interfere with normal family life and the child's pre-academic and social success.

When children who show Jamie's characteristics come from a dysfunctional family, it can be difficult to sort out an environmental problem from an organic one. A systematic management strategy can help shed light on the causes for the given behaviors. Often both environmental and organic problems are combined to create the difficult behaviors.

Finally, some children respond differently to the generic forms of ADD medication. Thus it's usually a good idea to begin children on the brand name and consider changing to generic forms after the success of the medication and the correct dosage have been established.

MARY

Thirteen-year-old Mary is in the seventh grade at a public school. She has been in the same school for three years. Prior to that, she attended a small private school where her mother taught. She was recently referred to a psychologist for assistance because of poor grades and a lack of motivation.

Both of Mary's parents are professionals. She also has two older sisters, both of whom do well in school. Mary plays the flute in the school band, plays soccer, and is a very creative and inventive child. Nevertheless she has shown inconsistency in her schoolwork—not doing homework assignments and projects on time, forgetting her responsibilities, losing things often, and exhibiting a general pattern of disorganization.

A review of Mary's past schoolwork indicates average to above-average scores on standardized tests, such as the Iowa Test of Basic Skills and the Cognitive Abilities Test. She received mostly grades of B and C at the private school she attended but has made mostly C's, D's, and an occasional F, since transferring to public school. Mary's poor grades frustrate her parents tremendously, since they have worked very hard to provide her with assistance and support throughout her school career. It appears that the demands of the upper grades are the main factors in Mary's decreasing grades, both on her report card and on tests. Her parents have tried numerous behavioral strategies and incentives at home. Over the years her teachers have also tried numerous interventions without consistent success. As a result of Mary's problems in school, she is also beginning to show increasing evidence of poor self-esteem.

Mary's psychologist recommended a trial on stimulant medication. She was begun on a dose of 20 milligrams of SR (sustained-release) Ritalin. Since Mary was not thrilled about the idea of taking medication, a contract was set up whereby she agreed to try it over a three-week period; at the end of that time, she would have the right to choose not to use it any longer if she thought it was not helping. Together with the medication, Mary started using a markerboard in her room to maintain lists of things she needed to remember and tasks she had to complete. She also began carrying a pad of "sticky" notes along with her to record items she needed to remember. She would attach these notes to the top of her books.

As a result of these interventions, Mary's productivity and attitude improved noticeably. She expressed an ability to concentrate better and understand more of what she was reading. An increase in her dose to 40 milligrams SR, coupled with an addition of fast-acting Ritalin, did not enhance her performance. Mary complained of headaches periodically, but according to her mother Mary is a hypochondriac. Her mother says that Mary has always complained of one ailment or another, but that the complaints rarely persist. This pattern of complaints subsided following the introduction of Ritalin.

Notes and Comments

ADD is particularly difficult to identify in adolescents. Because inconsistent behavior, changing priorities, and adjustment to physical changes are typical of youngsters of this age, many adolescents display characteristics that may lead others to suspect that they have ADD. In such cases, it is extremely important to review a child's educational history for indications that the characteristics were present *prior* to adolescence. This information may come from comments that teachers made on report cards in the early grades, from discrepancies between the child's standardized test scores and school grades, from reports by parents about the child's difficulty getting homework done and completing schoolwork, and from other sources. Even with this documentation, the child should currently meet the criteria specified for ADD relating to inattentiveness, impulsiveness, and distractibility.

Adolescents often feel invincible and have a difficult time admitting that they have problems. Consequently, many will resist the idea of taking medication and almost certainly will object to taking it at school. In such cases, the use of sustained-release medication is desirable. This avoids the need for a child to deal with the perceived embarrassment of having to take medicine at school and having to explain why she is taking it.

Finally, medication by itself is rarely sufficient treatment. This is especially true for children who have experienced many years of frustration and disorganization. It is necessary to help these youngsters learn techniques to become better organized and more efficient. Parents who have characteristics of ADD have probably learned some tricks along the way to help them be more successful. Sharing these strategies with their children can be helpful. Likewise, strategies that are recommended for children with ADD may also be beneficial to adults. In fact, an entire household can be made more efficient by strategically placing markerboards throughout the house. This helps all family members keep track of one another and of tasks that need to be completed.

THOMAS

Twelve-year-old Thomas lives with his grandparents. His parents were divorced several years ago. They were substance abusers who moved around often, and Thomas attended many schools before his grandparents enrolled him in a private school last year. He is currently in the seventh grade.

Teachers describe Thomas as a very likeable and athletic child. Nevertheless, they indicate that he is aggressive, impulsive, and has a hard time getting along with other children as well as getting his work done. At home Thomas is mildly defiant with his grandparents but has some chores around the house that he does regularly without having to be told many times. His grades have been marginal throughout his academic life, although his standardized test scores have always been in the high-average to above-average range. Apparently, the great importance placed on these tests by the school and family—or the way these particular tests are administered—has allowed Thomas to compensate and excel on these types of tests.

Thomas sees his mother occasionally and his father a little more frequently. None of these visits occurs more than once or twice a month, however. Thomas has spent most of his life living with his grandparents, who have tended to pamper him. He has no desire to live with either one of his parents.

Thomas was certainly underachieving and showed numerous symptoms of ADD. The first step in treatment was to initiate a daily report card to get a better idea of his day-to-day performance in school. When this strategy was explained to Thomas, he seemed eager to try it. An evaluation of his daily report card at the end of the first week was extremely positive. Thomas seemed to appreciate the structure that this approach imposed on him and enjoyed the positive feedback that he got from his grandparents on a daily basis.

After two weeks, when it was suggested that the daily report card be discontinued for a short time, Thomas balked and insisted on continuing the procedure. Thomas's grades and attitude have improved consistently over time, and problems at home have decreased, although there have still been a few episodes of defiance and rebellion, which is not unusual for a child his age. His grandparents now feel more capable of being consistent with Thomas, since much of the pressure to motivate him to improve his schoolwork has been taken off them.

Notes and Comments

Just as in Mary's case, a careful analysis of many factors is needed to untangle and understand Thomas's problems. It is clear that a nurturing and loving environment alone does not guarantee success. Children need structure and consistency; when these are absent, youngsters typically "ask" for these qualities in various ways. In Thomas's case, what appears to be a very complex and significant problem may have a fairly simple solution. Clear rules with clear consequences were what Thomas needed to bring his behavior and academic performance more in line.

ARTHUR

When Arthur was in the fourth grade, he did well on tests but rarely finished his seat work. His teacher would send home all of his unfinished papers; thus, in addition to the thirty to forty minutes of homework that she expected all of her students to do each night, she also expected Arthur to complete his unfinished papers. Unfortunately, forty minutes worth of homework for most fourth-graders took Arthur two to three hours. With his unfinished classwork added to the homework load, all of Arthur's time—and his parents'—was spent on homework. Life was miserable for him and for the whole family.

Arthur's parents met with his teacher on a number of occasions to discuss their child's problems, but the teacher said it was Arthur's responsibility to get his work done and that "maybe his parents shouldn't baby him quite so much." This infuriated and frustrated Arthur's parents, particularly since they had tried every strategy they knew to get their child working on his own. They used incentives. They tried spanking him. They sent him to his room. They took away his privileges. Nothing had worked.

Finally Arthur's parents were referred to a professional who recommended that they request a Student Support Team (SST) meeting. The parents recruited an advocate to accompany them to a meeting with Arthur's teacher, the school administrator, and a peer teacher. During this meeting, the school representatives expressed little sympathy for Arthur's plight. They warned his parents about how much more difficult things would be when Arthur got into middle school and how nobody would coddle him in the advanced grades.

The parents' advocate countered with a request that several steps, consistent with the recommended structure of SST meetings, be taken at that time:

- That Arthur's teacher and his parents describe the problem;
- That the teacher discuss her suggestions for how to

resolve the problem and that the parents describe strategies they had used at home;

• That the group agree that all logical approaches had been used to resolve the problem and that a modification of expectations for Arthur be made, given the fact that his grades were good and he appeared to know the work but had difficulty demonstrating his knowledge in traditional ways.

Notes and Comments

It is rare to find school professionals these days who have not heard of Attention Deficit Disorder. Unfortunately, there still are a few, and an even larger number who know about the disorder but are not willing to listen to the concerns of parents of a child with ADD or to make accommodations to meet the needs of these children and their families. This is what happened with Arthur and his parents in their attempt to get the school to respond to their concerns. In the end, however, the parents' advocate was able to negotiate a solution.

The advocate suggested—and Arthur's teacher finally agreed—that Arthur work no more than one and a half hours on homework and schoolwork on any night. At the end of that time, work would be put away and unfinished classwork would be sent back to the teacher. In addition—and, again, with great reluctance—the teacher consented to try other approaches in the classroom to help Arthur get his classwork done. She also agreed not to send home more than one classwork assignment each day.

As the year proceeded, as well as in subsequent years, Arthur continued to make good grades. Home life became considerably less frustrating and more enjoyable for the whole family.

At a recent two-year follow-up, Arthur was still having to spend a good bit of time doing his homework but appeared to be motivated and was earning good grades. Home life also continued to be less stressful than it had been in the fourth grade.

It is unfortunate when parents must seek outside help to pressure the schools to fulfill their responsibilities. Indeed, many school personnel are very committed to children and do everything within their means to assist. Sometimes this is not enough for children whose problems are severe or for whom other nonschool professional intervention is needed. Moreover sometimes the problem is so unique that outside resources are needed to provide guidance. But ADD is now recognized as a common problem, and schools must join with parents—rather than take sides against them—to do the right thing for the child.

MATT

Matt is a five-year-old who was adopted at the age of two. He was in foster care from the age of three months until soon after his second birthday. In his original environment, he suffered extreme deprivation. The foster home in which he lived for nearly two years was also a neglectful environment.

Currently Matt lives with his adoptive mother and his older sister and brother, both of whom were adopted from other families. The adoptive parents are divorced, and the children live with the mother. Matt is characterized as a combative child who is defiant toward authority and unpredictable in his behavior. His teacher says Matt has "fits" in school, where he is likely to throw a chair, knock everything off his desk, or attack another child when he is corrected or told to do something he doesn't want to do.

Matt is in a kindergarten class in a private school and shows problems staying on task and learning new songs and poems. He enjoys going to school but is unpredictable in his behavior once there. He shows language delays, particularly in the use of pronouns (for example, "Me want some") and has speech articulation problems involving sound substitutions.

When Matt came into the office for an evaluation, he wrote holding his pencil with a full hand grasp. When the evaluator tried correcting Matt's pencil grip, the child began fighting and tugging at the evaluator. "You're not taking it from me," he said. He called the evaluator stupid and kicked him.

During formal testing, Matt was cooperative but moved around a lot. On standardized tests, he scored high in spatial and math skills, but low in language and memory skills. Matt clearly met the criteria for ADD, although his history and current behavior suggested a more deeply rooted emotional disorder.

Given Matt's background of neglect, as well as his current behavioral and social problems, the evaluator weighed two options: an intensive psychiatric work-up or a short-term trial on stimulant medication prior to referral for additional services. The evaluator decided to recommend to Matt's physician a preliminary trial on medication.

Matt was started on a low dose of Ritalin. Reports from his teacher were instantaneous and positive. The change in Matt's behavior at home was also dramatic. His behavior was more consistent, he was beginning and completing his work more efficiently, and he was interacting in a more friendly way with other children. Matt and his mother continue to receive counseling, and Matt appears to be a much happier and productive child, showing only intermittent episodes of the type of combativeness that had earlier been a regular part of his repertoire.

Notes and Comments

There are no easy and definitive answers for the problems of some children with ADD. This is particularly true when the child's current behavior is complicated by a very significant past history. In such instances, critical and delicate decisions must be made to find the quickest solution to a problem without doing any additional harm.

Behavioral intervention programs to help children with severe emotional problems have yielded inconsistent results and often require long periods of time before progress is seen. Consequently, the decision to try Matt on Ritalin was made with the understanding that the trial would be monitored closely and was extremely unlikely to do him any harm. The benefits, however, might be significant.

Nevertheless, given the extensiveness of the problems, it is important that Matt and his other family members be involved in regular counseling with the goal of helping Matt and his family members deal with current and future demands.

SARA

Sara is six years old. Since she was old enough to walk and talk, Sara had been having severe temper tantrums, didn't sleep well, was a picky eater, and argued constantly with everyone. The intensity of her problems increased as Sara entered new social situations and reached dramatic proportions when she began kindergarten. All behavior management strategies appeared ineffective with Sara. Home life was chaotic—not only for Sara but for her parents and her three older siblings.

When Sara entered kindergarten, she was put on Ritalin. The medication was effective for a brief period of time; yet even at high doses it did not allow her to maintain enough self-control to function well in the classroom or at home. In addition, her appetite and sleep patterns remained poor.

After several months of adjusting doses and schedules, Sara began to exhibit eye scrunching and uncontrollable sniffing. Since these tics, it was felt, were the result of her medication, Sara was changed to Cylert. On this medication, she began rolling her eyes and clearing her throat a great deal, plus she continued sniffing. And while her behavior improved briefly at each dose level, improvement was never maintained.

Over several months, numerous meetings were held at school to change Sara's workload, to improve communication between the school and home, and to discuss other ways to evaluate Sara's progress. Finally it was decided that Sara would be taken off all medication for a period of time to see how she would respond. The tics decreased but did not disappear, and her behavior and productivity remained extremely inconsistent.

Sara was referred to a neurologist, who diagnosed Tourette's syndrome and began Sara on clonidine. The tics disappeared, and there was some improvement in her behavior. The dose of medication was eventually increased to the point where Sara was given a transdermal patch to wear. Unfortunately, she was not able to tolerate the adhesive from the patch and had to resume taking the medication orally.

Classroom and home modifications continued with modest improvements in work and behavior. Treatment then focused on reintegrating Sara into the family unit so that there was more enjoyment among family members, as well as less emphasis on Sara's problems and more emphasis on her accomplishments.

Notes and Comments

Many parents who have children with ADD will relate to Sara's story. Family life is never totally free from stress and anxiety. Some families experience continuous bouts with modifying behavioral approaches and medications, observing changes, and modifying and adjusting still more.

Sara represents one of approximately 10 percent of children with ADD who are resistant to most traditional interventions. Discovering what will help Sara be more consistently successful requires a delicate combination of factors. First, someone must be available who can provide suggestions and help monitor intervention—a type of case manager. Second, Sara's parents and teachers must be willing and able to apply behavioral interventions and to modify these fairly consistently based on their observations and other objective and subjective evaluations of progress. Finally, Sara must have medical services available that will consider the use of less traditional medical interventions when traditional ones are ineffective.

The side effects that Sara experienced from the various medications serve as a reminder that few medications are totally free from causing other changes that may be undesirable. When those changes are not life-threatening, the physician may closely weigh the benefits of the medication against the frequency and intensity of the side effects when deciding whether to continue with that medication. In all cases, whenever a new medication is prescribed or a dose is changed, parents must be especially vigilant for both undesirable physical changes in the child's behavior (e.g., rashes and eye blinking) and for complaints of discomfort.

When flexibility, consistent intervention, and good medical care are present, even children who appear to be resistant to treatment will show some benefits. Above all, good communication with the child is a necessity. That way, she will have a good understanding of both her limitations and the efforts she can make to improve her performance—and she can take pride in her accomplishments.

Appendix

Selected Books, Pamphlets, and Videotapes on ADD for Children, Parents, and Teachers

BOOKS AND PAMPHLETS FOR ADULTS

Barkley, Russell. *Attention Deficit Hyperactivity Disorders: A Handbook for Diagnosis and Treatment.* New York: Guilford Press, 1990.

Braswell, L., and M. Bloomquist. *Cognitive-Behavioral Therapy with ADHD Children: Child, Family and School Interventions.* New York: Guilford Press, 1991.

Conners, C. Keith. *Feeding the Brain: How Foods Affect Children.* New York: Plenum Press, 1989.

Copeland, Edna. *Medications for Attention Disorders and Related Medical Problems.* Atlanta, Georgia: 3 C's of Childhood, 1991.

Fowler, Mary Cahill. *Educators Manual.* Plantation, Florida: Ch.A.D.D., 1992.

Friedman, Ronald J., and Gut T. Doyal. *Attention Deficit Disorder and Hyperactivity,* 2nd edition. St. Clair Shores, Michigan: Interstate Printers and Publishers, 1987.

Goldstein, Sam, and Michael Goldstein. *Managing Attention Disorders in Children: A Guide for Practitioners.* New York: Wiley Interscience Press, 1990.

Gordon, M. *ADHD/Hyperactivity: A Consumer's Guide.* Dewitt, New York: GSI Publications, 1990.

Greenberg, Gregory S., and Wade Horn. *Attention Deficit Hyperactivity Disorder: Questions and Answers for Parents.* New York: Research Press, 1991.

Hechtman, L., and G. Weiss. *Hyperactive Children Grown-Up.* New York: Guilford Press, 1986.

Ingersoll, Barbara,. *Your Hyperactive Child.* New York: Doubleday, 1988.

Kennedy, P., L. Terdal, and L. Fusetti. *The Hyperactive Child Book.* New York: St. Martin's Press, 1992.

Parker, Harvey C. *ADAPT: Attention Deficit Accommodation Plan for Teaching.* Plantation, Florida: Impact Publications, 1992.

Parker, Harvey C. *The ADD Hyperactivity Handbook for Schools.* Plantation, Florida: Impact Publications, 1992.

Parker, Harvey C. *The ADD Hyperactivity Workbook for Parents, Teachers & Kids.* Plantation, Florida: Impact Publications, 1988.

Phelan, T. W. *All About Attention Deficit Disorder.* Glenn Ellyn, Illinois: Chud Management, 1992.

Robin, Arthur L., and Sharon L. Foster. *Negotiating Parent-Adolescent Conflict.* New York: Guilford Press, 1989.

Weiss, Lynn. *Attention Deficit Disorder in Adults.* Dallas, Texas: Taylor Publishing, 1992.

Wender, Paul. *The Hyperactive Child, Adolescent and Adult.* New York: Oxford Press, 1987.

VIDEOTAPES FOR ADULTS

Barkley, Russell. *ADHD: What Can We Do?* New York: Guilford Press, 1992.

Barkley, Russell. *ADHD: What Do We Know?* New York: Guilford Press, 1992.

Copeland, Edna D. *Attention Disorders. The School's Vital Role.* Atlanta, Georgia: 3C's of Childhood, Inc.

Garfinkel, B., and D. Cantwell. *ADHD Active Partnerships.* Minneapolis, Minnesota: University of Minnesota, 1990.

Goldstein, Sam. *Educating Inattentive Children.* Salt Lake City, Utah: Neurology, Learning and Behavior Center, 1989.

Taylor, John F., *Answers to ADD: The School Success Kit.* Salem, Oregon: Sun Media, 1993.

BOOKS AND PAMPHLETS FOR CHILDREN

Dixon, E., and K. Nadeau. *Learning to Slow Down and Pay Attention.* Annandale, Virginia: Chesapeake Psychological Services, 1991.

Gehret, Jeanne. *Eagle Eyes.* Fairport, New York: Verbal Images Press, 1991.

Gehret, Jeanne. *I'm Somebody Too.* Fairport, New York: Verbal Images Press, 1992.

Gordon, Michael. *I Would If I Could.* Dewitt, New York: GSI Publications, 1992.

Gordon, Michael. *Jumpin' Johnny: Get Back to Work.* Dewitt, New York: GSI Publications, 1991.

Gordon, Michael. *My Brother's a World Class Pain.* Dewitt, New York: GSI Publications, 1991.

Levine, Melvin D. *Keeping a Head in School.* Cambridge, Massachusetts: Educators Publishing Service, Inc., 1990.

Parker, Robert N., and Harvey Parker. *Making the Grade; An Adoles-*

cent's Struggle with Attention Deficit Disorder. Plantation, Florida: Impact Publications, 1992.

Quinn, P.O., and J. Stern. *Putting on the Brakes: Young People's Guide to Understanding Attention Deficit Hyperactivity Disorder (ADHD).* New York: Magination Press, 1991.

VIDEOTAPES FOR CHILDREN

Goldstein, Sam, and Michael Goldstein. *It's Just Attention Disorder.* Salt Lake City, Utah: Neurology, Learning and Behavior Center, 1989.

SUPPORT GROUPS FOR PARENTS OF CHILDREN WITH ADD

Ch.A.D.D. (Children and Adults with Attention Deficit Disorders) is a national support organization for information on Attention Deficit Disorders, with local chapters throughout the country. It provides a semi-annual publication, *Ch.A.D.D.E.R.*, and a newsletter, *The Ch.A.D.D.E.R. Box.* For more information, write or call Ch.A.D.D., Suite 308, 499 Northwest 70th Avenue, Plantation, Florida 33317; (305) 587-3700.

Daily Report Card—Elementary School

Name: _____ Week of: _____

★★★★★★★★★★★★★★★★★★★★★★★★★★★★★★★★★★★★★★

	CLASSWORK	BEHAVIOR	HOMEWORK*	COMMENTS	
M O N D A Y	2 ☺	☺	Letter review worksheet. Complete and return.	Parent's Signature:	**M O N D A Y**
T U E S D A Y	3		Letter review worksheet. Complete and return.	Parent's Signature:	**T U E S D A Y**
W E D N E S D A Y	4		Numeral writing. Complete and return.	Report Cards in folder. Return the envelope. Keep the report. Parent's Signature:	**W E D N E S D A Y**
T H U R S D A Y	5		Practice writing your name (first and last).	Parent's Signature:	**T H U R S D A Y**
F R I D A Y	6		No Homework.		**F R I D A Y**

* Stamp if yesterday's homework is handed in.

DAILY REPORT CARD FOR MIDDLE SCHOOL AND HIGH SCHOOL STUDENTS

Name: _____   Date: _____

CLASS	CONDUCT (Circle)	CLASSWORK (Circle)	HANDED IN HOMEWORK?	TEST GRADES	COMMENTS	T. INITIALS
Period 1	S U	S U	Y N			
Period 2	S U	S U	Y N			
Period 3	S U	S U	Y N			
Period 4	S U	S U	Y N			
Period 5	S U	S U	Y N			
Period 6	S U	S U	Y N			
Period 7	S U	S U	Y N			

DAILY CHORE CHART
Week of: _____

Martin, Age 8

DAY	CLEANS UP ROOM	READY FOR SCHOOL ON TIME	FEEDS DOG (1 reminder only)	BONUS	TOTAL
Monday	☆	☆	☆	Took out trash. + 25¢	$ 1.00
Tuesday	Threw everything under bed!				.50
Wednesday	☆	☆	3 reminders and still not done.	Went to bed quickly, no fuss. +25¢	.75
Thursday	☆	Argued over sneakers or shoes.	☆		.50
Friday	☆	☆	Overnight visit with friends.	Took out trash. +25¢	.75 PAYOFF
Saturday	☆	Helped vacuum and dust. 25¢	☆		.75
Sunday	☆	Picked up pine cones and pulled weeds.	☆	Washed car.	.75

Bibliography

Abikoff, H., and R. G. Klein. Attention-deficit hyperactivity and conduct disorder: Comorbidity and implications for treatment. *Journal of Consulting and Clinical Psychology*. 60(6):881–92. December 1992.

Adesman, A. R., and E. H. Wender. Improving the outcome for children with ADHD. *Contemporary Pediatrics*. 122–37. March 1991.

August, G. J., R. Ostrander, and M. J. Bloomquist. Attention deficit hyperactivity disorder: An epidemiological screening method. *American Journal of Orthopsychiatry*. 62(3):387–96. July 1992.

Barkley, R. A., G. J. DuPaul, and M. B. McMurray. Attention

deficit disorder with and without hyperactivity: Clinical response to three dose levels of methylphenidate. *Pediatrics.* 87(4):519–31. April 1991.

Barkley, R. A., M. B. McMurray, et al. Side-effects of methylphenidate in children with attention deficit hyperactivity disorder: A systemic, placebo-controlled evaluation. *Pediatrics.* 86(2):184–92. August 1990.

DiTraglia, J. Methylphenidate protocol: Feasibility in a pediatric practice. *Clinical Pediatrics.* 30(12):656–60. December 1991.

Elia, J., B. G. Borcherding, et al. Stimulant drug treatment of hyperactivity: Biochemical correlates. *Clinical Pharmacological Therapy.* 48(1):57–66. July 1990.

Fiore, T. A., E. A. Becker, and R. C. Nero. Educational interventions for students with attention deficit disorder. *Exceptional Children.* 60(2):163–173. October/November 1993.

Garfinkel, B. D., C. D. Webster, and L. Sloman. Individual responses to methylphenidate and caffeine in children with minimal brain dysfunction. *Canadian Medical Association Journal.* 113(8):729–32. October 18, 1975.

Goldstein, S., and B. Ingersoll. Controversial treatments for children with attention deficit hyperactivity disorder. *Ch.A.D.D.er.* 6(2):19–22. Fall/Winter 1992.

Greenhill, L. L. Pharmacological treatment of attention deficit disorder. *Psychiatric Clinics of North America.* 15(1):1–27. March 1992.

Hauser, P., A. J. Zametkin, et al. Attention deficit-hyperactivity disorder in people with generalized resistance to thyroid hormone. *New England Journal of Medicine.* 328(14):997–1001. April 8, 1993.

Heath, C. T., H. H. Wright, and S. R. Batey. Attention deficit hyperactivity disorder: Does it affect adults too? *Southern Medical Journal.* 83(12):1396–1401. December 1990.

Hinshaw, S. P. Academic underachievement, attention deficits, and aggression: Comorbidity and implications for intervention. *Jour-*

nal of Consulting and Clinical Psychology. 60(6):893–903. December 1992.

Kelly, D. P., and G. P. Aylward. Attention deficits in school-aged children and adolescents: Current issues and practice. *Pediatric Clinics of North America.* 39(3):487–512. June 1992.

Leckman, J. F., M. T. Hardin, et al. Clonidine treatment of Gilles de la Tourette's syndrome. *Archives of General Psychology.* 48(4):324–8. April 1991.

Liu, C., A. L. Robin, et al. Social acceptability of methylphenidate and behavior modification for treating attention deficit hyperactivity disorder. *Pediatrics.* 88(3):560–5. September 1991.

Pelham, W. E., K. Burnett, et al. Methylphenidate and baseball playing with ADHD children: Who's on first? *Journal of Consulting and Clinical Psychology.* 58(1):130–33. February 1990.

Pelham, W. E., K. E. Greenslade, et al. Relative efficacy of long-acting stimulants on children with attention deficit-hyperactivity disorder: A comparison of methylphenidate, sustained-release methylphenidate, sustained release dextroamphetamine, and pemoline. *Pediatrics.* 86(2):226–37. August 1990.

Pisterman, S., P. Firestone, et al. The role of parent training in treatment of preschoolers with ADD. *American Journal of Orthopsychiatry.* 62(3):397–408. July 1992.

Rapoport, J. L. Diet and hyperactivity. *Nutrition Review.* 44 Suppl:158–62. May 1986.

Rotta, N. T., A. Guardiola, et al. Efficacy of imipramine in children with attention deficit hyperactivity disorder. *International Pediatrics.* 6(4):343–46. 1991.

Safer, D. J., and R. P. Allen. Absence of tolerance to the behavioral effects of methylphenidate in hyperactive and inattentive children. *Journal of Pediatrics.* 115(6):1003–8. December 1989.

Shaywitz, B. A., S. E. Shaywitz, et al. Growth hormone and prolactin response to methylphenidate in children with attention deficit disorder. *Life Science.* 46(9):625–33. 1990.

Vincent, J., C. K. Varley, and P. Leger. Effects of methylphenidate on early adolescent growth. *American Journal of Psychiatry*. 147(4):501–2. April 1990.

Wender, P. H., and F. W. Reimherr. Bupropion treatment of attention-deficit-hyperactivity disorder in adults. *American Journal of Psychiatry*. 147(8):1018–20. August 1990.

Wender, P. H. and M. V. Solanto. Effects of sugar on aggressive and inattentive behavior in children with attention deficit disorder with hyperactivity and normal children. *Pediatrics*. 88(5):960–66. November 1991.

Wilens, T. E., and J. Biederman. The stimulants. *Psychiatric Clinics of North America*. 15(1):191–221. March 1992.

Zametkin, A. J., T. E. Nordahl, et al. Cerebral glucose metabolism in adults with hyperactivity of childhood onset. *New England Journal of Medicine*. 323(20):1361–66. November 15, 1990.

Zentall, S. S. Research on the educational implications of attention deficit hyperactivity disorder. *Exceptional Children*. 60(2):143–153. October/November 1993.

Index